A HIGH SCHOOL THEATRE TEACHER'S SURVIVAL GUIDE

A HIGH SCHOOL THEATRE TEACHER'S SURVIVAL GUIDE

Raina S. Ames

Routledge
Taylor & Francis Group

New York   London

Published in 2005 by
Routledge
Taylor & Francis Group
270 Madison Avenue
New York, NY 10016

Published in Great Britain by
Routledge
Taylor & Francis Group
2 Park Square
Milton Park, Abingdon
Oxon OX14 4RN

© 2005 by Taylor & Francis Group, LLC
Routledge is an imprint of Taylor & Francis Group

Printed in the United States of America on acid-free paper
10 9 8 7 6 5 4 3 2 1

International Standard Book Number-10: 0-87830-201-8 (Hardcover) 0-87830-202-6 (Softcover)
International Standard Book Number-13: 978-0-87830-201-7 (Hardcover) 978-0-87830-202-4 (Softcover)
Library of Congress Card Number 2005004714

Library of Congress Cataloging-in-Publication Data

Ames, Raina S.
   A high school theatre teacher's survival guide / Raina S. Ames.
      p. cm.
   Includes bibliographical references and index.
   ISBN 0-87830-201-8 (hardback : alk. paper) -- ISBN 0-87830-202-6 (pbk : alk. paper)
   1. Theater--Study and teaching (Secondary)--United States. I. Title.

PN2078.U6A43 2005
792'.071'273--dc22   2005004714

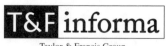

Taylor & Francis Group
is the Academic Division of T&F Informa plc.

Visit the Taylor & Francis Web site at
http://www.taylorandfrancis.com

and the Routledge Web site at
http://www.routledge-ny.com

Why Read This Book?

Often, theatre teachers emerge by default. They may be young English or speech teachers who participated in a few plays in high school. They may not be particularly comfortable being the extracurricular drama director, but by lack of seniority, the task falls to them to run a theatre program.

There may be theatre teachers whose only goal is to create the supreme high school drama department. They love teaching theatre and they thrive on directing plays; however, they didn't foresee the reality of teaching theatre plus other subjects such as speech or English.

This book is intended to serve as a guide for theatre teachers of any background experience. I spent eight years as a high school drama director and theatre teacher. I also taught English, speech, and television broadcasting. I know the demands of teaching while trying to hold together an extracurricular drama department. I have very specific ideas about the quality and shape of a high school theatre department, but the content is not meant to be prescriptive. This book is only meant as a guide to help teachers form their own programs. I know the feeling of floundering, and I only hope, as someone who has already been there, to give something tangible for drama teachers to help answer tough questions that arise during the curricular or extracurricular process. The text is short because I know a teacher's time is valuable. There is an extensive collection of appendices with lesson ideas, sample schedules, and resource guides. As an educator, I feel it is my duty not only to let others learn from my mistakes, but also to share what has worked for me. I had a mentor who said you are only as good as the things you steal; please feel free to use these ideas in your classroom.

Enjoy,
Raina S. Ames

Contents

Part I
Curricular High School Theatre / 1

Chapter 1: Developing a High School Theatre Curriculum / 3

Chapter 2: Discipline When Dealing with Students / 7

Chapter 3: Curricula/Texts / 11

Chapter 4: Parent Relationships / 15

Chapter 5: Administrator Relationships / 17

Part II
Extracurricular High School Theatre—Building an After-School Program / 19

Chapter 6: Extracurricular Program Responsibilities and the Value of Saying "No" / 21

Chapter 7: Scheduling and Time Management: Inherent Problems / 23

Chapter 8: Casting Issues / 33

Chapter 9: Discipline and Ethical Issues / 37

Chapter 10: Overview: Maintaining Excellence / 39

Appendices
A Course Syllabi / 43
B Board-Approved Class Proposals / 51
C Sample Schedules / 61
D Sample Audition Form / 73
E Class Assignments, Activities, and Lesson Plan Ideas / 77
F Lecture Notes and Handouts / 93

G   Sample Exams: History and Analysis of Theatre / 123

H   Sample Grading Rubrics / 131

I   Suggested Audition Pieces for Young Actors and Source Guides / 137

J   Three Character Analysis Ideas / 143

K   Technical Request Form / 147

L   Sample Press Releases: Short and Long Formats / 149

M   Computer Software / 153

N   Performance and Classroom Contracts / 155

O   Sample Parental Agreement Letter / 161

P   Resources for Teachers / 165

Q   Sample Blocking Notation / 173

R   Sample Shakespeare Script Cuttings / 177

Bibliography / 183

Selected Bibliography / 183

Index / 185

Acknowledgments

All I have come to believe about training high school theatre students has its genesis and superior example in the teaching of Maxine Joyce. Through her exacting standards and knowledgeable guidance at Macomb High School, I learned what it means to be a drama teacher. Mrs. Joyce influenced who I am both as a student and as a teacher of theatre.

Dr. Noreen Barnes gave me inspiration and confidence for the creation of this work. Many of the ideas in this book were sparked by stimulating discussions in Dr. Barnes's classes; her validation and guidance then helped me to shape my experience and understanding into a coherent form.

Both of these extraordinary women deserve thanks and praise for the positive influence they have had on all of their students. They are each a tribute to educational theatre.

Part I

Curricular High School Theatre

Chapter 1

Developing a High School Theatre Curriculum

SCENARIO

A father of a male student comes to you to ask why his son should be involved in that theatre stuff instead of sports. Do you have an answer?

Yes! Theatre is also about learning to be on a team. The intangible benefits of discipline, cooperation, and artistry are just as valuable as the knowledge we impart. Theatre layers its education and gives students a wealth of varied skills. Just as sports create a cohesive camaraderie among its players, theatre combines multiple skills and many different kinds of talent, putting forth a group-inspired piece of art. This unique experience brings just as much personal satisfaction and offers valuable outlets for those who choose theatre as their extracurricular activity.

In whatever discipline we choose to teach, as educators, it is our responsibility to prepare students for the level that is to come. All courses and activities have value, but many people do not see theatre as a "real" class. As high school theatre teachers, we provide a challenging curriculum that lays a firm foundation that prepares students to enter any college theatre program with integrity and a wide knowledge base. For those who say, "Many of my drama students are not going to be theatre majors," I say that your students will then have benefited from a program that has fostered self-discipline and appreciation of the arts that will enrich and color their life experiences from that point on. Challenge and quality in a high school theatre program will never be wasted on our students.

For those who were thrust into the position of theatre teacher, I understand your dilemma; as educators, we have taken on the huge responsibility of imparting knowledge. If we sign a contract with a district in which we agree to teach theatre even if it is not our forte, we have made a promise. In many districts, especially with speech and theatre, this will mean the students' only contact with this discipline is with you. Before signing that contract, it is imperative you recognize the magnitude of that promise. If you accept the responsibility, your charge is to provide a quality education. In addition, those trained in theatre who accept positions in other disciplines have a similar responsibility.

Many people look at theatre courses as the easy, throwaway classes, and it is difficult to combat this. Our best defense is to build a solid program. The first step should be to decide what you feel is important for students to know about theatre when they leave high school. A teacher's philosophy is a very personal thing, but I want to give you some ideas to think about.

If the purpose of education is to prepare students for what is to come, the obvious question is what comes next for high school students? There are three answers to that. Some students will become theatre majors, so their need for knowledge is immediate and obvious. Others may be going to college, but they are not going to be theatre majors. Still other students will not go to college. They will go either to trade schools or directly into the work force. Surely they will not need to know anything about theatre.

Here comes the part where you have to start formulating what you believe is the good of teaching theatre. Your principal will be the first in a long line who will ask you to articulate this. If your answer is simply, "I have to teach it to have this English/speech job, so I'll make it work," perhaps your philosophy needs some tweaking. Michael Brandwein is a motivational speaker who, in his seminars, demonstrates that teachers can teach any discipline. The work is about the motivation of students, and the subject matter has little to do with accomplishing that task.

Maybe teaching theatre is really the only thing you want to do, but the English/speech classes are the only way for you to even get close to that. Maybe you think you will suffer through those other disciplines until you can gradually weed them out and be teaching theatre only. You have to rethink that theory as well. There are very few schools where teachers teach only theatre, and the people who have those jobs hold on until they die or retire, so the rate of turnover is very low. The first step in your philosophy, whether you are born to teach theatre or are thrust into it, is to accept the responsibility for anything you were hired to teach. Then you need to make the conscious commitment to educate students as earnestly and creatively as you are capable of doing.

Next, you need to map out what concepts are important for students to know. If you study the history of theatre and its various periods, you see parallels to the development of literature. You also see historical influences on the emergence and disappearance of different periods. Theatre is one of the very few disciplines that combine several other areas of study. It is easy to see play analysis as literature, philosophy, psychology, *and* history. Teaching production aspects involves self-discipline, artistry, excellence, cooperation, group dynamics, and patience. Not to mention geometry, woodworking, art, and home economics. Theatre has the potential to prepare students for life. There is a wealth of material, but you as teacher must decide what will be emphasized. That choice depends on your specific school's needs (*see* Appendix A and Appendix B).

The standard high school program hopefully already has classes in place. Typically there will be at least one course; it may be a play analysis class for academics who want to learn more about theatre, but do not like to perform. Then there also may be a production class to introduce students to the elements involved in putting a performance together. This class is geared toward performance. If, however, your school only has one theatre class, you may wish to combine academic and performance assignments so all types of students are served.

The question still remains: what do you think they need to know when they leave high school? Let's start with the assumption that these classes would be separate. The way to start building that philosophy is to look at a list of the different periods in theatre history.

If you have little knowledge of this, there are several valuable resource books. You can also ask your local university or professors in your alma mater's theatre department to see what theatre history book they use, but an extensive overview of each period can be found in Oscar Brockett's *History of Theatre* (*see* Appendix P). After you look at the different periods, you can decide which major influences you would like to cover and from what angle. If you are not strong in history, perhaps you would like to take a different approach by concentrating on the literature of different periods and teaching theatre like an English course. Many anthologies of plays can be found starting from Greek theatre and moving through the periods, though you have to be aware that not all literary time periods match dates exactly with dramatic time periods. *An Introduction to Theatre & Drama* is a comprehensive collection of plays separated by different periods in theatre history (*see* Appendix P). At the beginning of each section, there is a brief discussion of the period and the historical influences. If possible, also try to include as many plays with young people as central characters to draw your students to the material. Bottom line, though: teaching new subjects is all about trial and error. You may rewrite this course two or three or ten times, but find what works best for you. When you start, though, I recommend having a solid plan. Even if that plan morphs into something you did not expect, at least you will have a solid foundation from which to work *(see* Appendix A).

When I taught "History and Analysis of Theatre," I saw this class as an upper-level English course that was designed to combine the analysis of significant works in the historical context of the different periods of theatre. I felt it was important for students to start with Greek theatre to see how it evolved; we then examined what historical and social influences affected the periods and the style of writing. I approached this as a college preparatory class, so analysis, synthesis, and evaluation were the most important skills I wanted to develop in my students. By critically analyzing texts and making comparisons to other works within the historical framework, I wanted students to have a scholarly understanding of theatre history, something we covered through lecture and discussion as related to the analysis of representative works (*see* Appendix F). I used essay tests so they had to think and evaluate what they were reading (*see* Appendix G). This was a rigorous approach, but these students were challenged, and they learned a great deal about theatre and history, which they could then apply to their further studies in World History and English. In fact, after some of my students graduated and they came back to visit, they said that the essay tests I gave helped prepare them for the rigors of college.

As the final project in my history and analysis class, I had students choose a particular period, pinpoint the specific play requirements of that time, and write a play in the style of that period. I stressed that quality was not the issue. They had to articulate what were the major criteria for a play of their chosen period and they had to demonstrate those criteria in the writing of a work that fit the time. This was a demanding yet creatively satisfying project for students, and it helped them get to know a theatre era in greater detail.

If you feel this assignment is too rigorous, you can lead students in other playwriting activities. TheatreVirginia, a professional regional theatre in Richmond, Virginia, ran "New Voices for the Theater," a statewide playwriting competition for Virginia students. When I was Director of Education & Cooperative Learning there, we held the thirteenth annual summer residency and festival for high school students. Our Playwright-in-Residence was acclaimed author and alumni of the program, Clay McLeod Chapman. He chose pictures of real people from the turn of the century who were living in Jackson County, Wisconsin. Through his guidance, students used these pictures as springboards for writing monologues. During the festival, this was perhaps the most prolific exercise; students created poignant, moving monologues that we then incorporated into a separate performance. You may still further simplify your use of playwriting in class by checking out the classroom playwriting ideas found in Appendix E. You see that students need not tackle entire units to exercise playwriting skills.

Turning to a theatre production class, you need to pinpoint what areas you feel are most beneficial to study. For example, in my last school, students were not allowed to go on the catwalk, so teaching lighting would not serve a practical purpose. Because I could not use students to set lights during actual productions, I did not highlight this. However, our program included student-directed one-act plays, so I spent a great amount of time having students create director's books and actually direct scenes for class (*see* Appendix E). Because as directors they are responsible for all aspects of production, I also focused on scene design and makeup techniques. In addition, we spent a great amount of time on acting both in monologues and in scenes. Students were required to do character analyses (*see* Appendix J), and they had to costume and block their scenes and monologues.

Because I often found that actors tended to have a superior attitude toward technicians, I required all actors to put in ten hours of technical work that usually translated into set construction. I felt this was of major importance, so I also covered set construction in my class. I always planned the show with the largest set to run concurrently with this class so students were getting practical experience working on a set from nothing to the final product. This served as a wealth of teaching opportunities for me, and because I was usually the set designer, much pressure was removed by being able to do some work during the school day. For me, the overriding philosophy for that class was to make it functional, so whether students were writing director's books or working on set construction, their work was immediately applicable to the production of theatre in real circumstances.

One of my best examples is the collaboration I had with the woodworking teacher at my first school. He was interested in having his students help with the sets to get practical experience in woodworking. We were able to work out a system in which he took his students to the auditorium during his class period and they would work on designs I supplied the woodworking teacher. It was one of the most stress-free experiences I have ever had dealing with set construction. Find any way you can to alleviate the stress that rests on your shoulders.

Teach to your strengths while best serving the needs of your students. Choose whether a literary- or production-oriented tack is more comfortable for you and start with this. Take classes at the local university to further your knowledge and to bolster your professional development requirements. As a bonus, the more classes you take, the closer you come to moving up on the pay scale. Start building a program based on courses that enrich your students' knowledge of and experiences in theatre. All courses will need to have formal proposals passed by the board of education (*see* Appendix B). Laying this groundwork will help save your sanity while providing rich, detailed theatre education for your students. Such comprehensive detail will help you define your own philosophies and procedures so you can justify the need for theatre education even to the most skeptical critics.

Chapter 2

Discipline When Dealing with Students

SCENARIO

You have taken over someone else's program, and your students are challenging your author-ity because you have replaced their favorite teacher. How do you build a positive working relationship with students without discipline problems?

SCENARIO

It is your first week on the job, and two theatre students feel you won't mind if they moon you at rehearsal. After all, we're all theatre folks. How do you deal with it?

Both of these scenarios awaited me at two different schools. The mooning happened my first year of teaching. I am five feet two, and I looked very young at twenty-six. Two stu-dents in a production thought it would be cool to moon me. They were at the top of the auditorium stairs, and as I rounded the corner I was greeted with their surprise. What can you do in this situation? The students laughed as they pulled up their pants, and I have to admit that, in my shock, I also laughed, but as a teacher entrusted with students, I had to respond appropriately. I talked with the other drama director, and then I went to the prin-cipal. Our show was opening in three weeks, but I had to establish a level of professionalism and trust with my administrator. The two students were suspended for 10 days; this meant they were gone for nearly two of the three weeks of rehearsal just before our show opened. This was when I learned the lesson that following the rules, though it may cause inconve-nience or distress to the play production, is more important. In the long run, students need to learn by teacher's example that making the hard choice may not be popular, but it is the only choice that should be made.

At another school, I came into a program in which the previous drama director was replaced because she was not a district employee and I was. She was extremely well liked by her students, and it was hard to come in after her. The students accused me, even before I got there, of kicking their teacher out of her job, so I entered the program with severe student skepticism and resistance.

I can tell you what *not* to do. Do not start out, as I did, staunchly going against every-thing the previous director did. I resisted many traditions she had set, and students do not react well to sudden change. I pushed them to accept my way of doing things far too quickly, and it was hard to win over the students and the parents. Taking your time to ease in your ideas for the program requires patience, and I wish I had heard this advice when I took that job. I ended up building a strong, quality program, but the road was rough in the beginning.

Every teacher has to find her or his own voice as a disciplinarian, but there are some standard truths that come to mind. Lee Canter is a wonderful reference for discipline. He suggests, through what he calls Assertive Discipline, that teachers express three or four guiding principles, warn of possible consequences, but also offer positive incentives the students could gain by following the guidelines for the classroom. I like this approach because it does not automatically presuppose students will misbehave (*see* Appendix N). Another helpful teacher resource book is *The First Days of School: How To Be An Effective Teacher* by Harry K. and Rosemary Tripi Wong (Harry K. Wong Publications, Inc.). It is a book not meant to be read cover to cover, but rather to be referenced based on need. It offers ways of setting up the classroom and the rules that govern your environment (see Appendix P). Whatever references chosen, though, teachers should never shut out the humanity in their classrooms.

One of the recurring conversations I have had with students has been their dissatisfaction with teachers who do not show them respect. Students often feel their teachers treat them with impersonal distance and condescension. Whatever style of discipline or classroom rules you choose, I would suggest basing classroom environment on mutual respect. There is an old but true saying, "Give respect to get respect." Students respond to teachers who take the time to treat them as individuals.

However, the trick is not to get too close. Especially as a theatre teacher. There is a fine line many drama teachers walk. If you look at our theatre discipline, whether in class, out of class, or both, we often spend more time with students than their parents do. As drama directors, we have ample opportunity to get to know our students; sometimes, we get to know facts about them we wish we did not know. It is the responsibility of a trusted teacher to maintain professionalism with students. The balance between appropriate and inappropriate behavior is very delicate.

Another problem arises. If drama directors know the students really well, how can they avoid favoritism? There will always be somebody accusing you of picking favorites. Teachers are human. There are going to be some students we automatically like, and there will be some who drive us bonkers. The more time you spend with students on extracurricular activities, the more you get to know their quirky eccentricities, and it is hard not to develop attitudes. The trick is to keep from showing them. If you look at drama programs, you can tell which teachers just want to be liked and which teachers wish to do quality work. I submit that if a teacher is able to get past wanting to be liked, he or she can more easily get down to the business of doing theatre. If you let go of whether the students like you or not, you can more easily stick to the constant standard of doing what is best for the program no matter what. Whenever a cast list goes up, no matter how much you have tried to be fair, you will be accused of favoritism, so you might as well do what will most benefit your production and let that idle gossip pass you by.

I had a particular student who wanted to be cast as a lead; she got angry when she was not given the role she wanted. She spent some time after rehearsal one day railing at me for having favorites. For nearly half an hour she emotionally laid out all the ways I had hurt her by "picking favorites" and not making her one. I had particular reasons why I did not cast her in the part she wanted, but she was not interested in hearing these. She needed to get this out, so I let her say her piece, and I listened. I was devastated. When students are so unhappy, I do feel bad about not being able to give everyone what they want, but the nature of a play does not allow for that. There is only one of each character, and I have to make a decision. I can make it based on favorites or I can make it based on what is best for the play.

The next year, this same student debated whether she should audition for a production because she thought I would never cast her after the tongue-lashing she gave me the previous year. When she did audition, she was absolutely the best person for one of the parts, so I cast her. If I were to cast by using favorites, I might not have put her in the play because we did not have the best relationship going, but she was absolutely what was best for the show. During that process, we both found healing, and I think we finally came to an understanding and appreciation of one another. I certainly am glad I did not let myself be personally wounded, because she brought much to that production.

I am not lauding my altruistic behavior. I have made plenty of mistakes as a drama director, but I am merely trying to make the point that consistency is the most important factor in dealing with students. I could have tried to be this student's friend and given her the part she wanted in every show, but ultimately this would not best serve our productions. In the long run, I believe I gained more respect from students because they knew above all I was concerned with excellence. They worked for what they got, and we produced quality theatre. It also helped them to see that I was serious about my work, and I was not running a popularity contest.

There is also a practical reason for having proper discipline in a high school drama department. More to the point, if you do not have proper discipline, you will lose respect from your fellow teachers. Even if you are the stodgiest, most no-nonsense person, once you say to someone, "I'm a theatre teacher," there is an immediate connotation. People's minds flash to pictures of wacky, off-the-wall behavior because it is assumed you have to be dramatic to teach theatre. It's almost as if theatre instructors are not considered real teachers. Indeed, it took time for me to establish credibility because my classroom was not a calm, orderly place; creative chaos and group interaction reigned in my room. Education is not supposed to be fun! Some people seemed to perceive that I must be questionable in my conduct.

I have seen plenty of teachers who blur the lines of appropriateness. Maybe they invite students over to their homes or they allow the students to swear and engage in crude behavior. Some teachers look the other way when students drink or smoke at cast parties or on field trips. This may seem like small stuff to some, but everything we do casts a keen eye on our integrity. To build respect for our programs, we must behave beyond reproach.

A drama teacher should not be a cool buddy. Students should be held to all of the school's rules, and it is not the drama director's job to undermine those regulations. You need that respect from your colleagues to get their support. Be mindful of how you decide to deal with student discipline. You are setting standards. Choose wisely and stay consistent.

I was often considered a "hip" teacher, and many students came to me to talk. Often, those students were perceived as my favorites, but I allowed—within reason—for students to get as close to me as they felt comfortable. I did not force the issue, so I did end up being closer to some more than others; however, even ten years later, the majority of my students with whom I still have contact cannot call me by my first name. Even a student who moved to Virginia and was in school at the same university where I was pursuing my Master of Fine Arts degree could only say my first name around others. When she had serious questions or topics to discuss, she reverted to calling me Miss Ames. I cannot explain that delicate balance; the best conclusion I can draw is that I treated students with humanity, I listened to them and valued their opinions and I made time when they needed to talk, but I always maintained a distance. They knew where the line was, and they did not cross or even push it. This was, however, completely unique to my personality and my experience. How I was as a teacher when I ended my high school teaching career is vastly different than how I was when I started. I learned by doing.

The kind of teaching assignments you are given can also change your discipline. If I had it to do over, I would not obtain certification for English just to make myself more market-able. Though I fell into teaching honors English and loved it, the bulk of my English teaching responsibilities were in ninth grade. I was not prepared for the type of discipline needed to deal with these students. Freshmen English students need far more structure than I was able to provide. As a teacher, I like to rely on mutual respect to maintain order in the class-room. Although freshmen reacted with appreciation when I attempted to let them have input on our class guidelines, they still were unable to self-govern enough to behave in the classroom. In fact, I would argue that because they liked and respected me, they felt more free to act out. My great plan backfired. I do not enjoy being the hard-nosed disciplinarian, but I was forced into that position two to three periods a day.

In a speech or drama classroom, there is more room for freedom. The nature of the curriculum allows for less structure, and I was much more at home in that environment. I was good at keeping people on track in that type of creative chaos, but the English classes really tested my endurance. Several times a day, I was constantly frustrating myself trying to keep students in their seats, minimizing bodily function jokes, and getting students to focus on grammar and literature. The frustration of that is what drove me out of secondary educa-tion. After eight years, I realized that if I were teaching drama only, I would still be a high school teacher; however, the more English I was given to teach, the more I felt trapped, so I got out to go to graduate school. Now I can pursue a career related only to theatre, and that has reenergized me.

This also serves as a lesson about choices I made when I began my teaching career. If I would have known then what I know now, I could have made wiser choices. I also would not have let the fear of never getting my first job push me into getting certified for some-thing I was not suited to teach. The bottom line: know yourself and how much you can handle. If you have reservations about teaching other subjects in addition to drama, listen to that instinct. You probably hold a reciprocal license, which means you can get certified in other states that honor your home state's certification, and there are states where you can find full-time drama positions. Knowing and setting your limitations at the beginning of your career will ultimately be the best thing for you and your students.

Chapter 3

Curricula/Texts

SCENARIO

Your principal has given permission for new theatre classes, but how do you go about choosing the right texts and curricula?

The most important step is to make a theatre curriculum that will be regarded as useful and necessary. Many people do not know what theatre teachers do. Even fellow teachers have a hard time thinking of theatre classes as nothing more than fluff. I also have had experienced guidance counselors who put troubled or struggling students in theatre classes because they thought it would be an easy grade. Whether you are in a district that already has theatre classes or you are writing your own curriculum, it is important that you make sure what you teach has value and merit. Maybe it is not the right thing, but it is a reality that theatre teachers have to justify their classes. Often, the drama courses are the ones that get cut first, so you need to build relevancy and respect for what you do with fellow teachers and administrators.

Where do you start? You need to plan assignments that are challenging and practically applicable to your extracurricular program. Let's start with a class that is an overview of theatre production. You need to ask yourself what are the most important aspects of theatre high school students should know. Acting is an obvious choice, but most high school students when they think of theatre only think of acting. It is important to expose students to the other roles in theatre so they have a more well-rounded view of theatre production. My experience was that my high school actors saw technical theatre as inferior. As a whole, they were not kind to technicians, so I wanted to change that by exposing them to the technical jobs of theatre production. Because of this, I emphasized scene design, scene construction, makeup techniques, and costuming. As I mentioned previously, students at one of my schools were not allowed to go on the catwalk because of insurance risks, so I did not emphasize lighting design or light hanging, but the concepts of color were discussed because they are part of the scene design process.

I also had another barrier to overcome. My last school had student-directed one-act plays every year, but at some point before I started teaching at that school, the students began to see these as a chance to push the limits and aggravate the administration. The theatre student behavior was blatantly disrespectful and antiauthority, so to help counteract that, I phased in a rule that any one-act director must first take the "Introduction to Play Production" class. In that course, students studied directing, made director's books for a scene, cast it, and directed it for a grade in class. Director's books included script analysis and stage blocking notations (see Appendix E and Appendix Q). After they were chosen to direct a one-act play, they had to make a director's book for the play and they were not allowed to go into auditions unless that book and their choice of play had been approved. After two years of this requirement, the students' productions showed marked improvement. They strove for quality over shock value. In fact, my principal caught me in the hall one day and said he really thought the class requirement had done a lot for improving the quality of the one-act plays. This credibility was priceless to me. It bought me more latitude and respect from my administrator, but it also required that I live up to his confidence.

The goal is to target what your students need. The play production class should be a supplement to your extracurricular program, but some possible areas of study are:

- acting
- directing
- stage managing
- scene design and scene construction
- lighting design, light hanging, and light focusing
- makeup techniques
- costume design
- props

If you do not have particular knowledge of some of these theatre aspects, students or professors from local universities often enjoy the opportunity to teach workshops at your school. Even if you do not have money for stipends, professors have service obligations as part of their tenure or promotion process, so you might get them to donate time. If you do not have a local university, perhaps volunteers from a community or professional theatre will assist you.

Of course you will want to teach acting. I found the best way to start is with improvisation and theatre games. Students need to reach a certain comfort level with expressing themselves creatively. There are reference books on acting and improvisation found in Appendix P. Maria Novelly or Viola Spolin's work is particularly effective with young performers. Next you will want to begin memorized acting pieces. There are debates as to whether monologues or scenes should come first. Because I want my students to first start focusing on character analysis (*see* Appendix J), I start with monologues. It is easier for students to work on the first assignment independently without the distraction of a partner. During this section, I would discuss the preparation of successful audition pieces (*see* Appendix I). This helped to strengthen the auditions coming into my after-school program. Then I worked on scenes. I eventually began giving students the choice of doing either a monologue or a scene for the final performance. I felt the ability to choose was important for my students' comfort level because live performance takes a great deal of personal risk. For all assignments, I gave students grading rubrics in advance (*see* Appendix H). I found that, even though it was still a subjective process, by having fixed numbers to add up and figure as a percentage, students were less likely to question their grades.

The other class that is often a good sell with administrators is "History and Analysis of Theatre." It is easy to push as an academic course and its value is priceless. Students of your extracurricular program can be immeasurably enriched by this course. A study of theatre history provides student actors with a context for the plays they are performing. The work they do in your class can enhance the work they do in the extracurricular drama program.

When teaching the course, I would recommend giving students as clear and complete a class syllabus as you can (*see* Appendix A). Not only does this make the parents feel better to see that their students will be studying specific areas, but it lays out the semester nicely both for you and for the students. I would recommend planning first in generalities, but if you start either a play production or a history and analysis class without making a scope and sequence of study, it is almost a certainty that you will run out of time. Map things out for yourself. If you want to do set construction, you should not cover this in a week. Think of the practicalities and what you can realistically cover in depth and with meaning. One way to accomplish this is to give students specific guidelines for assignments and grading (*see* Appendix H). It is hard to quantify theatre assignments, so clear parameters help set up specific, quality assignments.

After you have settled on the areas of study, you need to choose a text. Some standard high school theatre texts are *Play Production Today, Theater: Production and Performance,* and *The Stage and School* (*see* Appendix P). Schools have no lack of textbook advertising magazines, so you need to find descriptions you like. Next call the textbook company and say you are looking to adopt a new theatre book. You should request a free copy, a desk copy, so you can start to make your decision. Also ask to see any supplementary materials that might come with the text so you can evaluate if this book will be good for your class. In 1997, I chose *The Stage and School* above all the other texts I perused for one reason only: this book included scenes and monologues in the text, and these scenes and monologues were far less archaic than any other text I considered. This resource was very valuable to me because students when looking for performance pieces often would say, "I can't find anything." I could get them to sit down with the text and at least come up with a choice, and the pieces were not too long or difficult for young actors. However, since I left high school teaching, I found another play production text more comprehensive: *Theatre: Art in Action*, edited by Lisa Abel and published by National Textbook Company, was awarded the Distinguished Book Award by the American Alliance for Theatre and Education (*see* Appendix P).

As you are choosing a text, though, remember that schools often only adopt new texts every seven years or so. This choice has got to be one with which you can live. Even though it may seem overwhelming, make the effort to really compare texts so that you find the best book for your course. Otherwise, you will spend a lot of outside planning time trying to supplement a text that, when it comes, ends up not meeting your needs.

You may still wish to supplement your textbook with other materials. You will find it helpful to collect monologue and scene books. I kept a tub of books in my room. I had plays in there as well, and students found the variety very helpful. It was a personal expense, but I found the benefit to be worth it. In fact, the speech team students also used the books for resource material. When I left for graduate school, there was a day when students came in to visit the tub because they realized it would not be there for them the next year. Should a teacher have to provide her own materials? In a perfect world, no, but there is usually very little money for textbooks, so I chose to give that contribution to my classroom because it made the teaching process easier.

Chapter 4

Parent Relationships

SCENARIO

You have parents offering to chaperone events and give technical support for the plays, but you find out it is all a ploy to get their student a leading role in the next production. How do you handle that?

It seems like every parent thinks her or his child is the greatest. When serving as drama director, you can be exposed to difficult behavior. It would be nice to think parents would unselfishly give of themselves, and that very often happens, but there are also parents who harbor selfish interests. Very often, those parents are living vicariously through their child or they are trying at all costs to protect their child from disappointment. I have been burned on a number of occasions because I have preferred to see the best in parents, but it is wise to be wary until you are absolutely sure whether or not the parents have ulterior motives.

Here is the advice: do not ever give a role to a student as a favor or because of parental friendship. Once you embark on that trail, you have found the slippery slope. You cannot do such a thing without negative repercussions, so the best course of action is to keep your integrity and make casting decisions independent of parental pressure.

Your drama department cannot be based on quid pro quo. If you make that choice, you give parents power over your program. This is how it may start, though. You cast a student in a lead role, and the parents are delighted. They offer help with sets, costumes, or concessions, and you gratefully accept because you are swimming in the enormity of trying to produce, direct, design, and tech your show. The parent offers her or his home for the cast party, and then there might be an offer to chaperone a theatre event. At some point, you announce the next show, and then when the parent sees you in the community, somehow the conversation comes back to how perfect Jimmy or Jane would be for this or that role. You are reminded to call if there is any help this parent can offer for the next production. It is insidious. If you innocently accept the offer to chaperone, that sometimes is construed to be an unspoken consent to give the parents and student whatever is desired.

Am I saying not to accept the help? Absolutely not. You cannot do this job without assistance. I started putting requests for parental help on the parent contract that went home *after* the cast list had gone up (*see* Appendix O). This helped me begin to get a feel for who was sincere and who was angling for something. You start to learn who you can count on no matter what and who is going to be a fair weather friend.

There are many roles parents can assume to help with your program. During a production, you will likely be in the house or the technical booth making sure the show is running smoothly. Depending on your production, you could have fifty or sixty students backstage at any given time. Though they feel the responsibility to put on a good show, students also can be drawn into misbehavior. Parent volunteers are great chaperones. If you have parents with superior skills in woodworking, painting, sewing, or electronics, you have a fine recruiting base for set construction, painting, costuming, or lighting. Parents also might be eager to provide support and organization for concessions. For any parental involvement, I would recommend putting one parent for each category in charge of rallying the other parents. If you try to micromanage every aspect of the production, you will likely drive yourself crazy. Let parents help, but try to gently make it clear that such support does not automatically claim preferred casting for their child.

Whenever a cast list goes up, you invariably will be accused of favoritism, bias, or prejudice against actors—no matter what choices you make. All you have is the integrity of knowing you made your decisions based on pure motive, so I recommend not letting yourself get pulled into a manipulative parental web.

The longer you are in a program acting with integrity and producing quality shows, the more parents you will win over. Time is one of the greatest tests for your program. When my high school director left, she had been on the job for twenty years. She was an institution, and she was not questioned because people knew her shows were going to be outstanding. The reason they were outstanding was because she cast who was best for the part regardless of student desire or parental pressure. She had earned this stature through her solid work. Try to obtain this same level of respect through consistency and quality.

Chapter 5

Administrator Relationships

SCENARIO

Your principal has no drama background and has seen only a handful of plays in his or her life. There is little understanding for what you do or why it is valuable to students. How do you change your administrator's mind?

We have a responsibility first and foremost to our position as teacher in the district. We must be team players, and the irony of that sports metaphor is not unintentional. Any teacher of the arts is going to quickly find that sports dominate most high schools. As theatre teachers, we have to pick our battles. What do we fight for? Are we going to argue every point or do we compromise? We have an obligation to assess the community in which we live and we need to decide what is acceptable to our audiences. We also have an obligation to adhere to the wishes and directives of our administrators. This does not mean we do whatever they say. After all, the bulk of administrators do not understand the full scope of what we do as theatre teachers; it is, however, our job to educate our administrators so they understand why we make the choices we do. As a theatre teacher, you have to establish a baseline of trust, which means showing yourself as reasonable and cooperative.

My last administrator, a physical education and health teacher, freely admitted he knew practically nothing about theatre. Because he was my superior, though, I went to him to double-check decisions. I would tell him what I was trying to do, and he would make judgments. He was not unreasonable. If I had valid explanations, he would weigh the factors and then give me a yes or no. I took play choices to him before I announced the season. Even if he did not know the specific play or have the time to read the full script, the act of bringing it to him opened a channel of trust. Eventually, when I would bring him a script he would say, "I trust your judgment."

When I took students to the Illinois High School Theatre Festival for the first time, one of our student-directed one-act plays was chosen for performance. The principal thought this was the largest part of the festival and he was not sure we should go every year. I took the festival program and wrote a detailed summation of all the workshops, play performances, and college theatre audition opportunities that were available to students. I emphasized the fact that in three days the students were exposed to more than we could ever give them in a year of school. My principal thanked me for taking the time, because he had not understood the range of opportunities, and he supported our going on a regular basis.

Finally, the only sure-fire way to gain the respect and trust of your administrator is through time. You need to establish your credibility and integrity through the productions. If you make choices that are appropriate for students and yet bring about relevant and thought-provoking messages, you go a long way toward building a comfortable and trusting relationship with your administration. My advice is to play by as many rules as you possibly can so that when it really matters, you have more freedom to do what you feel is necessary.

For example, an auditorium in one of my schools was regularly rented to outside organizations. Often, my sets had to be built so they were movable because groups were in and out of the facility. Other schools also came in to give concerts, and they would have backdrops and risers to be set up. Many times, I had to rehearse in other spaces. This was not ideal, but by being cooperative and flexible, I was able to eventually get to the point where the principal would not allow the auditorium to be rented out for the two weeks before my performances. There were always little issues that would come up, but by being reasonable, I was able to win many of the skirmishes because my administrator wanted to help me succeed. I was not regularly a thorn in his side, so when I made requests, he was inclined to say yes. The only big fight I did not win was my bid to paint black the blond wood floor. I did not expect to win this one, but my administrator did not say no immediately. He considered my proposal, he took it to the superintendent, and then it was vetoed.

We even got to a point where our productions were given special recognition. When we did *The Diary of Anne Frank*, we were able to do a full-length performance assembly for the eighth graders who studied the play in class. For a principal who was very loath to take students out of classes, this was a big step. The next year, we did a one-act play about eating disorders. We performed this at a competition, but the principal felt it was an important message that the entire student body should see, so he added an all-school assembly where we performed our piece for the high school students. Yet again, we felt the victory, and I learned that being reasonable and flexible gets you much farther than being staunchly antagonistic.

Ultimately, administrators are not out to suppress the drama department, but theatre teachers often feel that way. I think it is just a lack of knowledge that keeps administrators at bay. Many cannot see what it is we do, but there is something concrete about gridiron battles and three-point plays. As a theatre teacher, it is your responsibility to make sure your administrator has as clear an idea of what you do in the theatre as what the football or basketball coaches do in their positions. You are all there to better the education of young people, so learn to work together. Administrators like win-win situations. If you show you are a team player, you have far less friction to deal with.

Part II

Extracurricular High School Theatre—
Building an After-School Program

Chapter 6

Extracurricular Program Responsibilities and the Value of Saying "No"

SCENARIO

You are a new teacher coming in as drama director. The previous speech coach still works as a teacher, but she has refused to continue coaching because the job takes too much time. Your principal pressures you to take the position because it's a lot like theatre anyway. What's your decision?

When I accepted my first job, I taught English, speech, drama, and television broadcasting. I became technical director for the fall show, director for the spring musical, academic decathlon co-coach, co-auditorium manager, and director of contest play. New, nontenured teachers often are overloaded. They make agreements either because they are eager to start their teaching careers or they fear an unwillingness to do extracurriculars will cost them tenure. If I had it to do over again, I would refuse extracurricular duties not directly involved with theatre. Because my first love and attention went to play productions, any other duty took a backseat. This was not fair to the students or the activity.

The problem is not really saying "no" to administrators. After you are on the job, you learn how to do this tactfully; however, when you have students come to your room multiple times a day saying, "Please, please be the speech coach. If you don't do it, we won't be able to have a team this year," suddenly saying "no" becomes a horrible thing. The guilt that builds is hard to deal with. Students are so good at getting teachers to do things they may not want to do. I cannot count the number of sausages I have bought because I did not want to say "no" to students. I finally made a rule that I would say "yes" to the first person who asked me and then I would buy nothing more.

You can say "yes" to some duty: sponsorship, chaperoning, or coaching, but you have to truly evaluate whether you have the time and desire to do the activity justice. When students convinced me to coach the speech team, I went into it saying, "You know the drama department is my first priority, so we have to work around those duties." I was already rehearsing three hours each night for plays and working on Saturday and Sunday to build sets, so it was not fair of me to make the speech students second banana to what I considered to be my art. I do not like speech competitions; I do not agree with the pressure these place on students and the false sense of good or bad their rankings give them, but I said I would be the coach in spite of my feelings. This was absolutely unfair to the students. I eventually cosponsored and then eased out of the duty all together, but I was giving students my leftover time, and they deserved better.

Saying "no" also saves your sanity. You cannot do everything. If you say you will chaperone every dance or sponsor speech team and the theatre group, you are really eating up what little free time you have. You cannot be an effective teacher if you are dragging to work because you have too many activities you are sponsoring. The old adage is true, "Too many irons in the fire and nothing gets hot." Give your time to one thing and you can improve your craft, but if you spread yourself thin, you stand a good chance of doing a mediocre job in many things. You will always have papers to grade, you will have rehearsals to attend, and you perhaps might want to have a life. I burned out after eight years of teaching (seven years was the quoted figure in the 1990s for the average length arts teachers stay in secondary education). Part of the reason I burned out was because I gave everything to the job and did not save anything for myself. I had no personal life. I went to school at seven o'clock in the morning and very often did not leave until eleven o'clock at night. Not only is this insane, it also is not healthy. You need to pace yourself, and the only way you can do that is to learn how to say "no." Practice this early and often.

Chapter 7

Scheduling and Time Management: Inherent Problems

SCENARIO

Your theatre students also want to experience other extracurricular activities that conflict with your rehearsal times. What is fair? How do you deal with this and still have a quality production?

You probably face scheduling nightmares trying to plan when to have performances. First find out the major district and state testing schedules for the students and plan around those. Then the key is to work well with the sponsors of every group involved in possible conflicts. Most auditoriums house theatre, choir, and band performances. The auditorium might often be used for all-school assemblies. As mentioned previously, in one of my schools, the auditorium was also rented out for non–school-related activities. There will always be some conflict or obstacle, but you have to plan and do the best you can to make the way clear for a smooth rehearsal process. This takes preplanning.

There are certainties on which you can count. Football season will take out not only athletes and cheerleaders, but also students involved in marching band. You will have games to schedule around, and students will be heavy into marching band competitions, so deciding when to have the play production is very important. I have tried scheduling the play for Halloween weekend, but this made the rehearsal schedule very rushed. The year I did this, I hit the ground running with auditions beginning on the first day of school. The standard fall play date was usually the third weekend in November. I would have loved to have had two weekends of performance, but there is almost no way to do that. Football games go head to head with the fall play, and if your school makes it into the playoffs, the season is stretched, and you have no chance of avoiding doing the two activities concurrently.

The best way to go is to plan the year's schedule with the input of the music, theatre, and sports people. At the last school where I taught, we had an activities director, and every spring the arts teachers sat down with him to make a preliminary schedule. It came down to looking at the athletic schedule and seeing how few students would overlap on any given weekend. In the fall, if there was a home football game one weekend and a cross-country meet the next, the better choice for a theatre production was the weekend of the cross-country meet. Because the meets and games are generally scheduled through a state organization far in advance, it makes the best sense to use those dates as your guide for when to do a play or not. If you ignore these realities, you will only be sorely frustrated during tech week and performances.

In the spring, the number of sports that seem to interfere skyrockets. You have track, tennis, baseball, basketball, and volleyball. Sometimes your school might have soccer or lacrosse. The spring is very packed, but in terms of the drama department, it often is better to do the annual or biannual musical in the spring. Your band director will not want to prepare a pit orchestra during fall marching band season, and your choir director will want to get through state competitions without also having to work on the musical. Truth be told, there is never a good time to do a musical with fifty or sixty students onstage, fifteen to twenty in the pit, and ten to fifteen backstage. Just by the law of averages, with such a large cast and crew, many will most likely be involved in at least one other activity at any given time, but not producing the musical would be an unacceptable choice. Even though the musical causes the most stress, you will find it is the most anticipated performance.

Let's assume you have a two-play season. In terms of picking dates for your spring production, my experience has taught me that April is the best month. Because our school did student-directed one-act plays in late January or early February, the last week in April always seemed to be the best choice. Going into May is not a good idea because you have prom and graduation festivities. Sometime in March or April, you typically can count on spring break; some schools even have a February break as well. This determination is unique to your personal taste, but I do not feel comfortable with less than ten weeks of rehearsal for a musical, so the final weekend in April seems to be the best. At my last school, I was also fitting the show time around band competitions and annual trips. I could either do the show in late March or in late April. Because I wanted as much time as I could get, I always chose April. All of this has to be arranged with every party involved. If you choose your dates independently from every other activity, you are asking for complications that could have been avoided. There is enough frustration to greet you as a high school drama director. Any time you can lessen the irritations, make sure you take advantage of those opportunities.

The amount of shows done in a year is based on district tradition, the strength of your core group of theatre students, your group's funding opportunities, and facilities availability. At minimum, a fall and spring play are desired so that students heavily involved in fall sports and other extracurriculars still may have a chance to participate in theatre activities in the spring; similarly, students involved in spring activities will have the same chance. Some schools also have a winter production. Often, this production is either student-directed one-act plays, or it is the contest play.

In many states, there are play competitions. There are extensive arguments for and against pitting one play against another and ranking them. Unless each school is doing the same play, there is really no way to compare a Molière farce with a melodrama with a realistic drama. However, if you win or get runner-up, contest plays help bring recognition to your school; administrators understand plaques and banners, so if you are looking to raise the profile of your program, investigate play competition in your state.

Sometimes schools do a musical every year. They are the most expensive venture, but they also can yield the most profit. I have encountered schools that would have an early fall play, student-directed one-act plays just before winter break, an early spring play, and a musical in May. Of course, every school's choice is based at least partly on funding abilities. Often a program is self-sustaining, using ticket sales to cover costs. Though it would be helpful to receive funding from the district, you might find that you have more autonomy over your program if you are not beholden to district monies. You are better off raising your own funds.

There are many ways to raise money, but you must make sure these projects fit into your schedule. You will probably receive several solicitations for fundraisers such as candy, sucker, or meat and cheese sales. You can sell advertisements in your playbills, and you may solicit business sponsorship for funding of specific projects or productions. Students also can organize dances, produce variety shows and dinner theatres, or run car washes.

If you have a strong core of theatre students, the parents can motivate the formation of a theatre booster club. First you will need an organizational meeting with parents, volunteers for booster officers, a proposal presented to the school board, and monthly meetings to maintain and generate support from your parent base. The boosters can be responsible for selling concessions, drama paraphernalia, pork chop sandwiches, or any other product that would be logical and well received in your community. Some booster clubs sell coupon books for area stores or they find businesses that will match funds that are raised. I know a booster group that sponsored an annual New Year's Eve party to raise money for the school's new state-of-the-art track. If you have motivated, influential parents involved, your booster club can produce amazing results.

To strengthen your program, you also can join the International Thespian Society. This organization, part of the Educational Theatre Association, provides import to your program, gives your students access to *Dramatics* magazine, theatre festivals, and provides college scholarship announcements and auditioning opportunities. By formalizing the organization, your students will gain more ownership and authority over the program by becoming Thespian officers and members; hopefully, they also will be more willing to take leadership roles for fundraisers. I never did a fundraiser without the commitment of my Thespian officers. They were in charge of running the endeavor and keeping track of organizational needs.

One caveat to this fundraising idea is that almost every school organization sells something and, unless you live in a large community, it might be difficult to sustain many fundraisers. However, if you investigate the selling options and let your students have creative input on choices made, you can maximize your profits. Just make sure you have the time and necessary workforce to make the project a success.

As you build your program, you will welcome more and more students. With these students, more and more scheduling conflicts will come. There are some things that can be avoided. Many sports, music, speech, and academic activities practice after school, so evening rehearsals seem to miss a lot of conflicts. When students have games or performances, these should take precedence over play rehearsal; flexibility with other sponsors and coaches will serve you well when you need reciprocal consideration. You cannot hope to have students be conflict-free unless, possibly, you are teaching in a performing arts magnet school; as your program grows, though, you can begin to encourage students to set priorities and make choices.

The reality is that students cannot do everything. They will have to pick activities and prioritize. When it came to work, I usually asked students to rearrange their schedules to not conflict with rehearsals. If students were in sports that frequently took them out of rehearsals, they had to deal with the fact that they would not be considered for a leading role. You still want students to be involved, but you cannot hold your rehearsal process hostage to a sports schedule. There have been some occasions in which I did not follow my own advice. I was convinced I could not do the play without a student or two who were also heavily committed in other activities. I made a deal to work around their schedules, and it always brought more hassle than I wanted. Students will begin to decide which activity is more important and set their priorities accordingly. It is a good life lesson, and it is necessary. Help students make healthy choices.

Some programs have a staff of people, and I have even seen a smattering of schools that had full drama departments. I have found that each state ultimately drives the amount of emphasis and support given to drama programs. However, most schools seem to lack the appropriate number of faculty to fully support the activities. If you are the only adult working the extracurricular drama program, make sure you allocate your time wisely. If you are not only the director but also the lighting designer, costumer, and set builder, you will have to find times for this work in addition to the lesson planning and paper grading you will need to do for your teaching. So where do you start?

The most visible place to start is with actor training. Youth theatre is a wonderful place to watch discoveries happen for your actors. They are just getting started in their acting process, and it is a thrill to be in on the growth process. There are many styles of actor training from Stanislavski to Stella Adler's emphasis on environment and finding the reality in character circumstances to Strasberg's Method, which includes emotional recall. There is an intricate process to actor training, and a course of study would be much more beneficial than the limited information I can offer you in this venue. A theatre teacher should choose any method of training very carefully to protect the mental and emotional stability of the actors. However, I do feel there is a process that young actors follow. New, inexperienced actors need a lot of specific direction on where to go, how to feel, and what direction to take a character. Often, these actors will ask you to give them line readings asking, "How do you want me to say it?" As students start to learn the necessities of blocking, movement, voice production, and the nuances of character development, they begin to rely less on you for specific direction. I liken this process to a closed fist that slowly opens. The hand starts tightly constricted, but as the fingers uncurl, you have multiple skills reaching outward and finding their own way. Students naturally progress from heavily directed instruction to self-initiated exploration.

In terms of technical aspects, you will want to first turn your attention to business management. As mentioned earlier, you likely will be in charge of your funds. Find out how much your organization has in the bank, how many different accounts you have, how much is generally spent on a production, which area businesses will let you charge to your school district's account, and how much is usually charged for tickets. You will have to budget for each production area, buy the lumber and building materials, buy or rent costumes, and get gels for the lights.

It is best to plan the set first and begin work on it right away. I always had Saturdays set aside for set construction. I was there from nine o'clock in the morning until five o'clock in the afternoon, and students who were cast were required to put in at least ten hours of set construction. Each weekend, I would have students show up and I would assign tasks to get the work done. Though this time devoted on weekends was inconvenient, I could not direct and have set construction going on at the same time. I found it more efficient to have a block of hours each week devoted to this task, so I chose Saturday work times. In the spring, I also used my play production class time to cover set construction with hands-on experience.

If you can hire someone else to do the set construction, by all means do so. The ideal: get a teacher or another adult to take on the job of set designer. My high school drama director forged a long-standing collaboration with the art teacher in the school. While she rehearsed the actors, he worked with students building sets. Because we had a separate scene shop, this was easily managed. If you have a local university, there may be theatre students looking for a small stipend. If you cannot hire someone else, the task will fall to you; if you are stuck doing it, find the best and most efficient way to get this work done. You will want to plan so the set is done a week or two before you open to have it ready for technical rehearsals, so buy your materials early.

If you can, try to get the art or vocational tech teacher to enlist as head of set construction. There is usually a stipend attached, and you can use the help. If your district does not offer stipends for theatre, talk seriously with your administrator and write proposals to your school board. If you give them concrete evidence such as time logs and job descriptions for separate duties related to a production, perhaps you can start to get money in the form of stipends put into the hiring salaries.

Still, do not expect to get rich running a drama program. Generally, it has been my experience that suburban schools with large corporations within their city limits and more tax money have a larger salary and stipend range. In my last school, I eventually was making $700 directing plays, $400 designing sets and lights, and $1,100 directing the musical. If you compare my highest salary with the $5,000 a head coach was paid, equity seems out of reach. However, my last school was in a fairly rural area. I got the impression I was well-paid compared with my nearby colleagues. In fact, many directed for no extra pay.

If your district will not pay for extra help, sometimes parents who work construction either as a vocation or an avocation may render their services if they are approached. Also keep track of those parents who offer support and do not be afraid to call for their help. Use all the assistance you can get.

When you do the costumes, you may be able to find parents who are willing to take on the responsibility. If so, all you will have to do is monitor the spending and keep track of receipts. I was fortunate for many of my high school teaching years to have a parent who was particularly interested in theatre and costume design, and she provided hundreds of hours or work on different performances. As a teenager I was forbidden to use my mother's sewing machine because I kept breaking the needles, so I needed outside assistance. This mother's help was both high quality and of great value to my sanity.

If you again are stuck with the job, try to do it in the least amount of time possible. If you are doing a period show, see if you can rent the costumes. There are several companies that regularly bombard the drama director with mailings. Also, if you have an annual high school theatre festival in your state, you should be able to collect literature from costume rental companies. Make use of these companies if you can afford it. If your undergraduate or graduate university or college is nearby, see if you can work out a deal to rent or borrow period costumes. If you have a modern show, you might be able to find all that you need at the Salvation Army or any other thrift store. I had students directing a piece from the 1960s, and they made use of a thrift store in town that specialized in 1960s paraphernalia and clothing for a very small price. If you want inexpensive character shoes or other dance supplies, Illinois Theatrical offers great deals for organizations. You just need to sign up as a school group and use the district corporate account to order. Bargains are out there. Start networking with other directors to find out their sources.

You will also need to arrange publicity. Most newspaper and television advertisements are costly, but you can send press releases via fax machine for very little money. Newspapers and radio stations will then announce your press release (*see* Appendix L). Sometimes you can get the newspaper photographer to come to the school to take rehearsal pictures that are published in the paper the week of your performance. Perhaps you can even convince the newspaper to do an article about your show. Every town newspaper is different, but often it will help promote local school activities. If the newspaper will not send a photographer, you can take pictures yourself and ask the paper to print them. Often, if you e-mail a digital picture to a newspaper representative, it takes little effort to add it to the publication. Of course, you will need to make contact with a sympathetic reporter. If your school or district has a newspaper, newsletter, or television or radio station, make sure you find out the due dates for announcements and include them in these media sources as well.

Flyers, posters, and programs may be ordered for a relatively inexpensive price through your school's graphic arts department. If you do not have such a department, ask the local printer for a special deal. When buying any supplies, be aware that most schools have a tax-exempt number. You will have to provide a copy of the tax-exempt letter every time you make a purchase, so having a store of photocopied letters in your filing cabinet will serve you well, and you will save money each time you make a purchase. Find out the official procedure from your administrator or district accountant. See Appendix M for computer software that is helpful in creating programs and posters.

When you are making the playbill, I recommend keeping track of the information as you go. After the casting is done, fill out the cast list. Keep track of crew members and people you want to put in the "special thanks" category. Have your program finished before you go into technical rehearsals. Not only will you be too focused elsewhere if you wait longer, but you also need to give the printer ample time. I recommend having your students check their names to make sure they are included and spelled correctly. Invariably, someone is forgotten, but if you take the time to have students proofread, if there is a mistake, they are less likely to be upset.

I also found it good politics to include, usually on the back panel of the program, a listing of district administrators and school board members. I listed them in this order: superintendent, assistant superintendent, principal, vice principal(s), administrative secretary, school accountant, custodial staff, and the school board. The custodian, secretary, and the accountant will likely do much work for you. When you need a check more quickly than usual or need to make last-minute scheduling changes, people in these positions will be the ones who will pull you out of a jam. Presents are good, but program recognition is a small way to thank them.

In terms of lights, if you have an auditorium with stage lighting, plan your gel colors early because an order usually takes ten days to two weeks to get to you. Find out from a university lighting designer in your area which companies he or she uses and which seem the most reasonable in price and delivery time. You have to schedule time to cut the gels, put them in the gel sleeves, put those in the lights, and program all of your lighting cues. When you do start writing cues, it would be best not only to have your stage manager there to write the cues in his or her prompt book, but you should train as many students as possible to use your lighting and sound equipment so you are not stuck with the task of being the expert. At one point in my last school, I was the only one who understood how to use the new lighting computer system our district had purchased, so not only was I the one programming lights for my plays, but I also was called on to help with choir and band concerts for the district. If you teach students how to do this, you can lessen your load, and eventually you might have students who are proficient enough to do the cue writing for you so you can be freed up to take care of other problems.

The bottom line is the show dates will not change. You have a finite number of days to make everything work. You want the show to look as professional as possible, so it takes planning. To get students ready, I suggest requiring lines to be memorized one week before you really want them to be done; I also recommend making call times five minutes before you want to start and breaks being five minutes shorter than you really desire because it generally takes students five minutes past the due time to get themselves together and on stage. During rehearsals, maximize your time as much as possible by breaking down scenes into subscenes so not every student has to be there for the entire rehearsal. If you can have a specific schedule, you will lessen your frustration with rowdy students hanging around, and the students on stage will likely be more focused. Parents also will appreciate not being kept waiting in the parking lot. When you are doing a musical, if you have the space, I recommend having the choir director and choreographer working in separate rooms while you are working on acting scenes (*see* Appendix C).

When dealing with the technical needs, get started early and know exactly what you have to accomplish in how much time. After you have the plan, start delegating as much as you can. Ask parents to help with set construction, costuming, or lights. In the school where students were not allowed to go on the catwalks, I often asked parents to help. Again, see if your budget will allow you to hire university theatre students or professors where possible. Since I was in control of my budget, if I had excess money, I could pay people directly from the theatre account. The standard rate accepted by outside help was about $500.

Remember to maximize the use of your students as well. I usually included on the audition sheet a checklist of crews students would be willing to join if they did not get cast. Often, students still wanted to be involved in the production even if they could not be on stage, so student crews were invaluable (*see* Appendix D).

Crews also helped me give up dictatorial control and make the production more of a learning experience. You will want to have a trusted, organized student as your stage manager. At auditions, you will need someone to organize and herd the actors so the process runs smoothly. When casting, I also let my stage manager have input, and he or she would help organize the scheduling conflicts of all top choices. Before we settled on a cast, we had to make sure we could have the leads meeting at the same time. During the first stage of rehearsal, the stage manager should be writing down blocking and any subsequent changes so there is one definitive source for the actors' question, "Where am I supposed to be." After you are through the blocking process and actors start going without their scripts, the stage manager should then serve as the prompter. As you approach technical rehearsals, the stage manager should be organizing crews, getting final props lists to the property manager, taking and giving notes to designers, and getting his or her cue book ready for technical rehearsals.

All cues for lights, set changes, curtains, and sound should be called by the stage manager. I started my career in complete control, and the stage manager sat back watching me work during performances. This is neither fair nor an optimal educational experience, so I began training stage managers how to call a show. If you have never had the experience or do not know how this process works, ask someone from a university theatre department to train your stage manager. When I was in high school, our director hired a lighting designer from the university who also trained the stage managers how to run technical rehearsals. After you have a student who can do this, you then can assign younger actors to be assistant stage managers. They will be assigned duties from the stage manager, and during the run of the show, they can be deck managers who work backstage making sure set changes happen on time and actors get to their appropriate places. As the stage manager ages out of school, the assistant stage managers can be tapped to take over.

I have had many good stage managers, but I was especially fortunate to find a student as an eighth grader who joined our crew as a props person. She went on to be assistant stage manager and became enamored of the job a stage manager does. She bought Lawrence Stern's book, *Stage Management*, and learned everything about stage manager's kits, how to deal with auditions and rehearsals, and setting up crews. She took very seriously the requirement that stage managers remain neutral and not be drawn into the fights and drama that occur within a cast. She was my spring stage manager for three years, and she was the best role model for all other students who wanted to stage manage. In fact, others respected her so much, they said they wanted to work to be just as good as she was. This sort of self-motivation and peer training is invaluable for a theatre program.

When assigning a property master, you will want to find a very organized student. I found the mathematically inclined students enjoyed making databases for where props needed to be, when they were on and off, and which side of backstage should be the starting place for all props. Students who enjoy arranging are very well suited to this job. If you have a property master, one of your assistant stage managers can be an assistant to this person during the run of the show.

You will need students to run the light and sound boards. Usually, these pieces of equipment are housed in your technical booth. If you do not have one, you will need these people either in the back of the house or immediately offstage, depending on where the boards plug in. If you do not have equipment, sometimes a university department will lend equipment or you can always rent from stage lighting and theatrical supply houses. Either way, you will want crew members who can focus and be quiet, because the only people talking should be the stage manager unless there are problems or the tech operators who are acknowledging their standby cues. I also have found that if the stage manager is in the booth with lights and sound, the students in the booth do not have to answer over the headset, thus cutting down on radio chatter. Radio Shack sells radio headsets for around $50 each, and they work well within a theatre. You will just need to see if there are certain places (far backstage or near microphone receivers) where the headsets have a problem transmitting.

I had many students lined up wanting to learn how to use the electronics. I got to the point where I put together a tech club. These students were the core of our technical crews for productions, but I also trained these students to write light cues and set sound levels so they could be used to run outside events that rented our auditorium space. Any group that needed help filled out a tech request form (*see* Appendix K). I assigned the appropriate number of technicians; they were in charge of meeting with the groups, writing cues, and running the event. This alleviated the stress on me, the only district employee who knew how to run the equipment. These students also took ownership of the technical aspects of theatre, and this only strengthened my overall program.

I have found there are many students interested in being the makeup artists for shows. If you have a cast of fifty, you need people working assembly lines putting on makeup. I personally do not like using a lot of makeup in shows, especially on the men. Foundation serves a corrective purpose, removing faults in the skin. If you put foundation on men, they start to look like Ken dolls. I prefer just using a bit of rouge and some mascara unless we are doing a musical or character makeup. Makeup books are listed in Appendix P.

If you have a large costume show, you will want students to help with changes. Often the makeup crew can also serve as costume changers. If you make a crew responsible for the dressing room areas, you may have them hanging up costumes and putting them away as the play progresses. Students always want to get out to the lobby to see their friends and family, and it is often hard to corral them again to get the dressing rooms cleaned, so a crew helps alleviate the mess.

One year I had a student who was extremely interested in costume design. She had been working at the local university's summer stock theatre helping in the costume shop for many years and she was a very proficient seamstress. She showed interest in designing, so I let her work on the two shows of her senior year. She designed both costume plots and made whatever costumes we needed. She took on a straight play and a musical and she did a wonderful job. This took the pressure off me, and it enabled us to get the job done more economically because we were not allowed to put students on the district payroll. In addition, this was an excellent learning experience for a student who was going to be a theatre major.

When using student crews, the only caution I give is that whenever you put someone in an authoritative position such as stage manager or designer, make sure you keep a handle on peer dynamics. Some students can go overboard with their sense of power and drive the other crew and cast members crazy. It is difficult to find students who can stay balanced and remain neutral, but it is imperative that you train students well regarding this area. Otherwise, your crews will be ineffective, and your production values will likely fall apart.

Whether it is students, parents, hired help, or colleagues, find people who can fill the void for your shortcomings in theatre production and let people help you. In the beginning of a play process, do not lose track of parents who offer their help. Even if they are just helping with concessions or bringing food to feed the cast during tech week, set all of this up in advance. Give yourself as much help as you can get. It will save you time and stress.

Chapter 8

Casting Issues

SCENARIO

You have a sophomore and a senior up for a lead role. The sophomore is really the better actor. What's the choice you make?

Casting is really contingent on your objective for the drama program. If your objective is solely to introduce students to theatre production, you might choose to spread the wealth around and give everyone a chance to be on stage. If you are looking to push the envelope for quality in high school theatre, casting takes a different focus. A successful production is largely dependent on good casting. Directors have to make hard choices. If your sophomore is really the better actor for the part, you have to choose to cast the best actor or make concessions and give the part to the upperclassman because of seniority. Both philosophies are valid, and both offer rich opportunities for students.

When making casting decisions, you have to decide what qualities in each character are most important to you. Sometimes body type might not mean anything to you, but then there might be roles in which you feel body types are very important. When I directed *The Diary of Anne Frank*, I felt the families needed to look as realistic as possible. I wanted the children to look younger than the parents, and I also wanted to assemble families that looked right together. I had a good actress, but she was especially tall and looked very German. Even if I cast her as Miep, she was too tall to fit into the picture; however, the next year when I directed *Guys and Dolls*, not only was this same actress a stand-out in her audition for Adelaide, but I loved the fact that she was quite a bit taller than the young man we were casting as Nathan. Often Adelaide is cast as a more petite woman; however, I loved the juxtaposition of Adelaide having a greater physical stature but when it came to getting what she really wanted, a marriage with Nathan, she was powerless to make it happen. I then cast a very tall Sky and a shorter Sarah to be foils for Nathan and Adelaide.

In one show I went with the norm, but with the other I played the opposite. Both decisions were based on what I felt was best for each show. When it comes down to it, all casting is very project-specific and based on director preference. I would recommend, in whatever decision you make, that you be able to articulate and defend your choices in case you are called on to do so. Also choose a set of guidelines for casting and stay consistent with them regardless of student or parent reactions. Whenever you put up a cast list, someone will be unhappy, so you should be able to defend your choices.

One way to defend your choices is to ask other teachers to sit in on the audition process. Whenever I directed a musical, the choir teacher was part of the casting process. In straight plays, I often still asked the choir director to sit in. I also would ask friends of mine with theatre backgrounds to give me another eye. Casting by committee just helps you protect yourself. It is harder for people to cry prejudice or favoritism when you are not the only one making the call.

Whatever precautions you take, be prepared to still receive criticism. During one of the musicals, we cast one girl over another, and parents had complaints. Fortunately, a parent of one of the other theatre students was involved in the process, and when she was in a social situation where these parents were complaining about our choices, she was able to pipe up and defend us saying, "I was there. So-and-so was better than your child." This does not necessarily squash the behind-the-back complaints, but it does give a sense of reassurance in our choices.

I do not mean to make it sound as though there is always angst when casting, but you do have to be prepared for backbiting. The competition is always stiff for the women because there are always more female actors than male actors. There are far fewer young men who audition, so more of them get cast. I also have found that young men, though they get disappointed, snap back more quickly and do not hold this against you.

You probably also will face accusations that you precast. Actually, it would be foolhardy to choose a play completely oblivious to the fact you have no actors who could play the roles. You start with who you think your pool of actors will be and you make sure you can cover each lead role. If you are comfortable that you have at least one actor per role and you like the play, you have a winner. Auditions, however, never cease to surprise me. Although I might have an idea who would be good in a role, there are always students who sneak up from behind and take a part away from an actor. I love these surprises and I enjoy making the unconventional choice. When a new talent comes along, I like fostering that talent.

It is wonderful to bring in new students who are not part of your core theatre group. Often I would have athletes wanting to join in the fun. I always told my male students that the football or basketball court was not a place to meet women. If you come to the theatre, they are everywhere! And audiences love to see the star athletes acting, dancing, and singing. Burly guys tap dancing or doing *West Side Story*–type leaps is quite a sight to see. It also is a great box office draw.

In addition, sometimes I needed to supplement my casts with other people. Often there is just not enough male actors for all of the parts, so this is when you can get creative. I have cast teachers and community members, but my favorite was when I cast the superintendent as the book voice in *How To Succeed in Business Without Really Trying*; the assistant principal was tapped for playing Wally Womper in that same show. The book voice is offstage with a microphone, and Wally Womper only appears at the end of the play. Casting the man responsible for discipline in our school and having him tap dance and sing a solo added buzz about our show. As an added perk, I had built-in backstage chaperones that were a great source of support for our production.

When dealing with casting issues, you will have to evaluate how often you will use the same actor. You will probably have handfuls that are more naturally gifted than other students, and they will consistently win more roles. This will be perceived as favoritism, but keeping a consistent policy will be your saving grace. Even if you repeatedly cast certain actors, you gradually add less-experienced students, much like folding flour into cake batter. With this method, your newer actors will learn from the veterans, and you will slowly build up a stronger, cohesive core of actors. Let the suppositions about your motives pass you by.

As I have said before, you could choose to make casting decisions based on doing return favors for parents, but you have to think long and hard before going down that road. You open yourself for people attacking your integrity, and we all know teaching does not pay much, so the only thing we really can cling to is our integrity. Keep that precious and truly know what you are doing before you give that away.

You also will have to decide if you will use understudies. I understand that casting understudies enables a director to include more students; however, I have never been a fan of understudies. I feel it sets up an inherent rivalry where the understudies are hoping the leads will get sick or injured so they can take over. Sometimes directors have one or two understudy performances in which the leads take the chorus parts and the understudies get a chance to shine. I believe that casts form a cohesion and balance that is disrupted if actors trade roles for performances. We also only had three or four performances, so I was content not to use understudies. I instead preferred to use one actor per character. If a student became ineligible or sick, I would rather choose an understudy when necessary than having one from the start, even if the replacement had to use a script during the performance. In this scenario, it would be prudent to make it clear to your understudy that the lead could get better or off the ineligibility list; it is imperative, to avoid hurt feelings, that you make sure your student understands the uncertainty of signing on as the understudy, whether you have him or her from the beginning or on an as-needed basis. Of course, there are pros and cons to either choice; as director, you have the final say, so you need to make sure you are comfortable with whatever decision you make.

There are also other considerations when casting. You may have students you would love to cast, but they are booked solid with other extracurricular activities. At my second school, policy dictated that all extracurricular activities would be after school instead of in the evening. Students prioritized and only joined a few activities during the year. At my first and third schools, however, rehearsals could be held any time directors deemed appropriate, and students rarely narrowed their choice of activities. This led to many students overextending themselves. You might have swimmers, runners, and football, softball, baseball, basketball, or tennis players. Because of the after-school sports practice schedules, you most likely are already pushed to have your rehearsals in the early evening. I found at my last school, the best time for rehearsals was from six o'clock to nine o'clock in the evening. I did rehearse after school until six o'clock in the evening on Fridays, but overall, night rehearsals conflicted with the least amount of students; however, often games or practices will run past six o'clock, so the decision has to be made whether to cast students who have conflicts. Students also work, so how do you deal with it?

It is always best to have standards set before students audition. On the audition sheet, I always had students read a disclaimer and sign their acknowledgement of having seen it. I have included a sample in Appendix N. It may seem excessive, but I came to this through trial and error and lessons learned from, as one colleague called it, the school of CYA: cover your ass. It would be nice to live in a world where we could trust that students would not take advantage, but that unfortunately is not the case. During my first year, students took advantage of the fact that I did not have an established attendance policy for rehearsals. Students would say, "I have to work, so I can't be there." Pretty soon students were saying they needed to work, but I got word they were going out with girlfriends or boyfriends, so I began calling their place of employment to confirm that they were actually there. Yes, this took time on my part, but it let the boss know when students were using their work as an excuse, and it let the students know I was not going to let them take advantage. After that first production, you can bet I began making more specific guidelines. Students need that structure.

I eventually came to a point where I decided students could only have two unexcused absences. There are days when students would be sick from school, and because of school policy they could not come to rehearsal, so I would not hold this against them. If students attended classes that day but did not show up to rehearsal, if they had no valid excuse, their absence was considered unexcused. When they had two unexcused absences, I reserved the right to replace them. I did this quite often. In fact, there are more plays in which I replaced actors than in which the original cast remained intact. This action communicated many things. It taught that actor about responsibility and discipline, it told the other actors I was absolutely serious about the policy, and it established a level of professionalism I was pleased to have.

Chapter 9

Discipline and Ethical Issues

SCENARIO

You have a student who comes to you with personal problems and asks to talk. How do you handle this?

To this scenario I would say, "It depends on who the student is and what problem was brought to me." Ethics in teaching is a gray area. A teacher should never step over the bounds of appropriateness, but there are many lines that are blurred. Suppose a student is having "significant other" problems. He or she is not comfortable talking to parents or the counselor, so you are the chosen candidate because you spend so much time with the student and you are the theatre teacher so you will be understanding. Living as a teacher in a high school environment, you become quite aware of love relationships. You might spend a great deal of time helping students through bad breakups.

There are other more serious issues.

I had a student who was given a letter by a friend. In that letter, the friend described how she wanted to kill herself. My student did not know how to deal with this himself, so he pulled me into the issue. Of course, I was worried about his friend, so I asked to see her right away. I told her I had seen the letter and I wanted to talk. I spent almost two hours talking things out with her, and because I had her as a student in one of my classes, I knew her quite well. I was able to connect to her and talk about her feelings, but ultimately I had to tell her that I was legally obligated to report this to the counselor. The student was very concerned that her mother not find out, and her pleas were desperate; it is hard not to give in and let it go, but if she would have done something to herself and I had not reported it, I would have been legally and ethically responsible.

There are choices you make as a teacher. As a drama teacher, you do get to know your students on a deeper level than most other faculty. You spend time in class and in rehearsal with students. You get to know them as people. You see the romances they go through, you hear their hardships, and sometimes you become a counselor and a confidante. You may not want this role, but it develops nonetheless. Whether a correct perception or not, and most likely because of their extended contact, most drama teachers are considered one of the few who care about the students. This is an honor and a burden. You cannot abuse this status by doing anything unethical, but you also have choices to make. If your lead is upset by some personal problem, do you ignore it or do you deal with it because it is affecting rehearsal?

I had a student who asked out one of the actresses in our play. The day before we opened, he told a friend he was breaking up with her. It, of course, got back to the young lady, and the show was put in jeopardy because she was mad at him; in addition, they were awkward in the romantic scenes they had to play together. I was furious with him for leaking the information he knew would get back to his girlfriend. When they started dating, I begged him not to break up with her until after the show. Because it was so close to opening, he could have waited three more days, but he stirred things up in what seemed a very callous way.

This student came to me about midway through the year. He thought, based on his actions in the previous show, perhaps I would not cast him again, so he wanted to see if he should even bother auditioning for the spring show. We spent almost two hours discussing how we felt about the situation. I laid out all of the things he did that made me mad, and he laid out his feelings about my actions. He also gave me background on his life that led to certain character traits he had exhibited during the fall show. It was an intense revelation, but I felt this was necessary for us to deal with if we were going to have a future working relationship. He trusted me with personal information, and I was able to get a greater insight into who he was. This insight helped me look past his actions to his motivations, and it made him tolerable and even likable to me.

When he auditioned that spring, he turned out to be the best person for the lead, so I cast him. Since we had dealt with our animosities midyear, I was confident we could work successfully and professionally together. Would I spend that much time alone with every student? No, but these things are judgment calls. You know what your motivations are. Mine were to get to the bottom of what seemed like a student's mean-spirited behavior and help him to see how he could have acted more appropriately. We came to an understanding with one another that strengthened our relationship as teacher and student, but I know there are some students I would not be able to have this level of honesty with because it would be misconstrued.

Another dilemma arises. As you begin to get to know your students and they you, do you cover for them in class if they do not turn in assignments on time? Do you write them excuses if they are tardy to a class that will give them a detention that will interfere with your rehearsal time? As a drama director, you want things always to move smoothly, but as an educator, the bottom line is that you are trying to help these students be better human beings. If you enable their behavior, what favors are you doing them? Yes, a student in detention is an inconvenience. You may not agree with detentions—they may seem like empty, punitive exercises to you—but if this is the rule of your school, do you uphold it or flout it because you think it is ridiculous? You can choose to be the student's friend and do favors, but when he or she leaves high school and go on to other things, where is the safety net then? You are setting the students up for ultimate failure if you get them used to special concessions; sooner or later, they will not have anyone there to help them out. Hard lessons learned early help students mature more quickly to make their own rational, adult decisions. The beauty of being a drama teacher is that we are fortunate enough to see students as they make these life discoveries. They are not just endless faces funneling through. We are part of our students' life education.

Chapter 10

Overview: Maintaining Excellence

SCENARIO

You have a choice between a lesser-quality play that will bring in box office receipts and an American classic such as The Crucible *or* The Miracle Worker, *but it may not yield as much money. What do you choose?*

SCENARIO

You have a chance to build your own program. What should be the focal points of your drama department? What is most important for students to experience?

What is best for the students? This is a matter of personal opinion. I learned my teaching strategy from Maxine Joyce, retired drama teacher and director. I had the unique opportunity of being hired as drama director at my alma mater, where I was able to uphold the legacy I was given by my high school drama teacher. She spent twenty years in high school theatre, and when I began teaching she sat me down and said, "Don't do crap." I understood this to mean that I should not underestimate what my students are capable of accomplishing. If I repeatedly gave them poorly written but popular plays, I was devaluing their potential. Some of Mrs. Joyce's greatest productions included Aristophanes' *The Birds*, *The Importance of Being Earnest*, *Brigadoon*, and *The Crucible*. She retired in 1986, and people are still talking about her productions. A local university theatre professor once said Maxine Joyce was the best director she had seen. Never did the phrase, "It's good for high school theatre" enter into the equation. Having worked under Maxine Joyce, I know she was exacting and demanding, but she always gave us a sense that anything was possible. Because she did not give us limits, we did not create any for ourselves.

During my eight years of teaching at high school level, one phrase I hated the most was "That was a good production…for high school." One prepositional phrase holds such negative connotations that limit the possibilities in high school theatre. The problem is not with the audience, but with theatre teachers who adopt this philosophy. There needs to be a call to excellence that is led by high school directors. Whether focusing on process or product, it is possible for high school students to create quality theatre, but they must be given the tools and the encouragement to achieve excellence.

If education truly is supposed to be a building process, and each level is viewed as preparing students for what is to come, then we should be giving students challenging, quality dramatic material so they are ready to enter university theatre programs. High school theatre can be more than a steady diet of melodramas and comedies. Many schools do comedies because they think the shows will be easier to perform. In reality, producing good comedy is very hard, and you also want to expose your students to a variety of genres. The best balance is alternating box office successes with educationally varied literature. Even if students are not going to continue in college as theatre majors, they will certainly benefit from exposure to different styles and periods of writing. Whatever career path they might pursue, students will always have the varied experience of theatre that will forever enhance and broaden their knowledge base.

Stella Adler, renowned acting teacher of the twentieth century, said it was her goal to make students independent from the teachings of any instructor so they could learn to work on their own. In high school, theatre teachers should be approaching their programs with the same philosophy. Open that fist and let students flourish in a fertile and creative environment. Instill excellence in students by giving them more freedom and responsibility. Whether it is giving the stage manager control of the show instead of doing all of the work yourself, training self-confident performers, or building student-directed productions into the season, it is important that students are given a chance to be responsible for all or part of a production.

Theatre instructors need to decide what their goals are. Decisions have to be made about what basic skills should be learned by the time students leave high school. Just as elementary education feeds into secondary education, secondary theatre education should feed into the next level: university education; however, the reality is that students can go to college drama programs unprepared, but this does not have to be the case.

High school theatre teachers need to broaden instead of narrow their scope of expectations for students. I have been told that high school theatre students should never perform Shakespeare. Why not? Therein lays a wealth of teaching opportunities: students in most secondary curricular educational settings are made to read Shakespeare, and it is well acknowledged that Shakespeare is meant to be seen and not read. If students are prepared with a properly edited script and basic acting guidelines for Shakespeare, they will easily find success (*see* Appendix R).

When I directed *Much Ado About Nothing*, twenty-one of the thirty people participating in the production were new to high school theatre, and all of them were being exposed to the performance of Shakespeare for the first time. Beyond this, though, there is one other reason that stands above all others to justify my production. I cast a student who, the year before as a sophomore honors student, read this play in class with me. She was constantly frustrated by the language; by the end of the unit, she had declared Shakespeare "stupid." Nevertheless, she auditioned, and I cast her. After the production, this student came to my classroom very excited. She happily declared that she understood Shakespeare after being in the play and she loved it now. She took out *The Complete Works of Shakespeare* her mother had at home, and she was reading different plays on her own, understanding and appreciating them. It proves the point Oscar Brockett, well-known teacher of theatre history, made. He maintained that the primary goal of education ought to be "to put students in the position to become their own teachers so that teaching and learning are fully merged."[1] Even if the play had not been a success in any other area, this one student's conversion and enrichment was worth the process. That is what theatre in secondary education should be.

One production that completely transformed everyone involved was *The Diary of Anne Frank* by Frances Goodrich and Albert Hackett. When I announced I was doing this show, many of my colleagues and parents offered raised eyebrows. Some even expressed their thoughts: "Can students handle the maturity?" "Will they really do the piece justice?" Adolescents are underestimated much of the time. How could they possibly have the depth of feeling needed to portray the story of Anne Frank? I submit that students will reach great heights if we refrain from telling them they cannot.

The cast did copious research about their characters. We had a lock-in at our school's auditorium in which we worked on costumes, rehearsed, watched *Schindler's List*, and bonded with one another. Students did several improvisations to get into character, but the most effective was when I had those portraying the two confined families stand in a dark hallway leading to the catwalk. I had those playing the Nazi soldiers bang on doors and yell in German. The two actors playing Miep and Mr. Kraler led the two "families" from the auditorium through the inner classrooms in the school, and the "soldiers" were hot on their trail. They were led outside and back in again, and we then discussed the feelings they had. Ultimately, this experience was so potent for the students that they asked if they could start every performance in the hallway and be led to their places by Miep and Mr. Kraler. They also requested *not* to have a radio in the dressing room. When they asked if they could stay in character and have no talking while they got ready, I was terribly shocked but extremely proud of their dedication and professionalism.

The cornerstone of successful teaching is getting students to take ownership of their education; my actors had proven that they could perform with grace and maturity. They took on this story as a mission, and this play affected many people. Community members sent e-mails of congratulations, student audience members were impressed, and a woman who was not a mother of any cast members was so moved, she wrote a personal note to me and to every actor.

There is no magic in what we did. The reasons we were able to succeed depended on several factors that can be employed by any director at any high school:

1. I chose quality material.
2. As director, I had a strong attachment to the story.
3. I empowered the students by putting my belief in their abilities.
4. I challenged the students.
5. They challenged me and took ownership of the play.

We did not just put on a play; we found a truth that we cared about telling to the audience, and nothing was going to get in our way. This is what theatre can be about.

The play does not have to be based on a real story or be dramatic to be challenging. The key is not to underestimate the ability of your students. High school actors are hungry for performing, and they do not have a belief that some plays are out of their reach unless they are made to think this. Of course, the drama teacher must choose works responsibly, but there is no reason we as high school theatre educators have to settle. There are many dramas and comedies of great quality (*see* Appendix P). When students do not have limits placed on them, they have the freedom to explore and grow.

Yes, a drama director must have knowledge about directing and acting. Yes, it takes time for students to build up their skills and talents, but the alternative is accepting mediocrity. Students have the will to excel when that fire is fed by a positive, supportive teacher who continually challenges them. Drama is a very powerful medium. There is a wealth of learning students can glean from being involved in high school theatre. When you accept the job to be drama director, expect and welcome the responsibility for shaping students in a discipline that encourages depth of feeling and sensitivity. Take this mantle with pride, and do whatever is necessary to keep challenging the students as well as yourself.

Reference

1. Burnet Hobgood, ed., *Master Teachers of Theatre* (Carbondale: Southern Illinois University Press, 1988), 44.

Appendix A

Course Syllabi

Introduction to Play Production

GRADE COMPONENTS

1. Monologue performances
2. Duet scene performances
3. Set design and construction
4. Spring play audition
5. Makeup morgue
6. Improvisations
7. Quizzes/tests
8. Rehearsal scores
9. Director's book
10. Directing scene
11. Daily warm-ups

All prepared performances will require signup for performance dates. Anyone missing his or her assigned date with an excused absence will make up the assignment in class **the day of return** unless we have moved on to another assignment; in that case, all assignments will be made up before or after school within two days of the absence or the student forfeits the grade. Because you knew your due date before you were absent, there is no extra time. **All truancy automatically earns a zero.**

Anyone present but not prepared to perform will receive a zero, no questions asked. This is an **elective** performance class. You need to meet deadlines and take responsibility for your assignments.

SAMPLE GRADING SCALE

100+	A+
94–99	A
92–93	A-
90–91	B+
84–89	B
82–83	B-
80–81	C+
74–79	C
72–73	C-
70–71	D+
64–69	D
62–63	D-

Quarter grades are based on total possible points.

The semester exam is 20% of the final grade.

Expected performances/activities: Improvisations, acting monologues/scenes, directing scenes, makeup morgues, set construction and painting, final performances (both monologue and improvisation), final written exam.

History and Analysis of Theatre

Ms. Ames

Grading Components

1. Lecture notes
2. Discussion participation
3. Quizzes/tests
4. Research notes
5. Midterm analysis paper
6. Technology project
7. Original playwriting project
8. Final play draft and written final exam

All assignments are due on the day assigned; any late work will receive one grade letter penalty per day it is late.

	SAMPLE QUARTER GRADING			GRADING SCALE	
				100+	A+
Quarter 1:	708/740	96%	A	95–99	A
Quarter 2:	726/750	97%	A	92–94	A-
				89–91	B+
	SAMPLE SEMESTER GRADE			85–88	B
Q1 × 2	96 + 96 = 192/200			82–84	B-
Q2 × 2	97 + 97 = 194/200			79–81	C+
FE × 1	84% = 84/100			75–78	C
				72–74	C-
	470/500 = 94% A-			69–71	D+
(Final exam is 1/5 or 20% of semester grade)				65–68	D
				62–64	D-

Expected Plays: *Oedipus Rex; Everyman; As You Like It; The Importance of Being Earnest; Riders to the Sea; Death of a Salesman; The Glass Menagerie; Oh Dad, Poor Dad, Mama's Hung You in the Closet and I'm Feeling So Sad.*

History and Analysis of Theatre

ITBS Testing

DATE	IN-CLASS WORK	ASSIGNMENT
8/25	Introduction/rules/books/projects	
8/26	History Notes	
8/27	History Notes	
8/28	History Notes/Greek Theatre: *Rex*	*Read 10 pages from class* *Do handout questions*
8/31	DUE: Quiz and *Rex* questions DISCUSSION: 8/28 reading	*Read to end of play* *Do handout questions*
9/1	DUE: *Rex* questions DISCUSSION: 8/31 reading and *Medea* comparison	
9/2	**Medieval Theatre**: *Everyman* Begin reading/discussion in class	
9/3	Finish reading *Everyman* DISCUSSION: p. 79: 1, 2, 3, 4, 6, 8, 9, 10, 11, 5, 7	
9/4	Computer program/midterm/final project examples and discussion Brainstorm ideas	
9/8	LIBRARY: midterm work	
9/9	LIBRARY: midterm work	

9/10	**Renaissance Theatre**: *As You Like It*	*Read Act II, do handouts*
9/11	DUE: *As You Like It* questions DISCUSSION: Act II, dramatic structure/plot	
9/14	Read Act III: discuss and do questions	*Read Act IV*
9/15	DUE: *As You Like It* questions DISCUSSION: Act IV	
9/16	Read Act V: discuss and do questions	
9/17	DISCUSSION: presentation of play	

*****TEST: Greek to Restoration dramatic structure (notes and plays)*****

9/18	Comparison: **Restoration Drama** *Tis Pity…, Country Wife, She Stoops…*	
9/21, 9/22	*Much Ado…* and *Midsummer…* video portions	
9/23	TEST: Greek/Medieval/English Renaissance vs. Restoration	
9/24	Return tests/classroom work: Midterm Projects	
9/25	**Kabuki/Noh video**	
*9/28	**Seventeenth- and Eighteenth-Century Drama:** *The Miser*	
	Read Acts I and II	*Do handouts for I and II*
*9/29	DUE: I and II questions	
	Read Acts III, IV, V	*Do handouts for III, IV, V*
*9/30	DISCUSSION: Politics and Molière's plays	
*10/1	**Nineteenth- and Twentieth-Century Drama:**	*The Importance of Being Earnest* *Do Act I handouts*
*10/2	DUE: Act I handout Read Act II	*Do Act II handouts*
10/5	Read Act III: discuss and do questions	*All questions due*
10/6	DUE: All *Earnest* handouts DISCUSSION: Comparison/contrast: *Earnest* and *Miser*	
10/7	MIDTERM/TECHNOLOGY/FINAL PROJECT WORK	
10/8	Read *Riders to the Sea*	*Finish reading and do handouts*
10/13	DUE: *Riders* handout questions DISCUSSION: length and merit/dialect	
10/14	**Realism: Politics**	
10/15	Movie: *Death of a Salesman*	*Do handout questions*
10/16	Movie: *Death of a Salesman*	
10/19	Movie: *Death of a Salesman*	
10/20	Movie: *Death of a Salesman*	
10/21	DUE: all question handouts DISCUSSION: production vs. written work	
10/22	MIDTERM WORK	
10/23	DUE: midterm paper at the end of the period	
10/26	*The Glass Menagerie* (movie: beginning–scene 4)	*Do handout questions*
10/27	Read pp. 430–445	*Do handout questions*
10/28	Watch movie scenes	*Do handout questions*
11/2	Read end of play Watch end of movie	*Do handout questions*
11/3	DUE: all handouts DISCUSSION: merit/dramatic structure/theme	

11/4	FINAL WRITING OR TECHNOLOGY PROJECTS	
11/5	**Modern Drama:** beginnings/cultural influences (relation to *The Glass Menagerie*)	
11/6	Read Act I: *Raisin* Do ACT I question in class	*Read Act II, 1 & 2* *Do Act II questions*
11/9	DUE: handouts so far done Read and discuss: ACT III to end	*Read leftovers* *Do handout questions*
11/10	DUE: all handouts DISCUSSION: Theme/cultural implications	
11/12	**Absurdism:** *Oh Dad, Poor Dad, Mama's...*	*Read pp. 489–end* *Do handout questions*
11/13	DUE: handout questions DISCUSSION: theme, absurdism purpose	
11/16	DISCUSSION: **Modern Theatre's evolution** = potpourri	

*****TEST WEDNESDAY*****

11/17	DISCUSSION: **Musical Theatre's evolution** = *Les Mis* tape, soundtracks	
11/18	TEST: Seventeenth- and eighteenth-century drama; nineteenth- and twentieth-century drama; absurdism; REALISM; modern; musical	*First daily check of projects*
11/19	Return tests TECHNOLOGY PROJECTS: daily check	
11/20	TECHNOLOGY PROJECTS: daily check	
11/23	Final writing or technology projects: daily check	
11/24	Final writing or technology projects: daily check	
11/25	Final writing or technology projects: daily check	
11/30	Final writing or technology projects: daily check	
12/1	COMPUTER LAB: Final writing or technology projects: daily checks	
12/2	COMPUTER LAB: Final writing or technology projects: daily checks	
12/3	COMPUTER LAB: Final writing or technology projects: daily checks	
12/4	Rough drafts of final writing due at the end of the period	
12/7	Revisions and pairs comments: daily checks	
12/8	Revisions and pairs comments: daily checks	
12/9	Revisions and pairs comments: daily checks	
12/10	Revisions and pairs comments: daily checks	*Final drafts due*
12/11	DUE: final drafts end of period	
12/14	Read original plays	
12/15	Read original plays	
12/16	Read original plays	
12/17	Read original plays	*Technology projects due*
12/18	DUE: technology projects–beginning of period Read original plays	
1/4	Read original plays	
1/5	Read original plays	
1/6	Read original plays	
1/7	Written criticism	
1/8	Review	
1/9	Review	
1/12–1/14	Final exams	

Playwriting Project

1. Choose a period of Theatre History
2. Write a play in the style of that period
   a. Adhere to all theatre conventions (only the five-act rule can be forfeited)
   b. Recommended length: not less than twenty pages double-spaced and not more than thirty
   c. Two rough drafts due
   d. Revision and final draft due
3. Writing in class will periodically be provided throughout the semester so that students may ask questions along the way; eventually you will have three full weeks in class to either finish your manuscript or work on the technology project.
4. This play is the project component of your final exam; you will also be taking a cumulative written exam over the historical periods in theatre.
5. We will have play readings in class (two a day) so each script has a chance to get constructive criticism and be fine-tuned by the group. You can revise a final time and turn in a finished copy for extra credit.
6. All plays must have the following:
   a. Clear conflict
   b. Theme
   c. Dramatic structure
   d. At least two characters

Technology Project

Purpose: To use computer technology to create a step beyond a pen to paper project. The point is to stretch your creativity and increase your technological skills.

1. You may work in pairs (but you only get one grade; choose someone you know will pull his or her own weight).
2. Choose a particular event, theatre, person, or period from Theatre History.
3. Design a webpage with facts about a period in history (if you don't have a URL address, you may use mine); computer-generated costume replicas or theatre floor plans; make a virtual project such as the "Virtual Renaissance" I will demonstrate; use Hyperstudio to create a computer-generated assignment about one or several periods in Theatre History; create a database that catalogs the important similarities and differences of all the Theatre History periods; create a database of websites that pertain to a certain period of Theatre History. *Your own creativity is the limit.*
4. Approve the project with me.
5. Be sure to be inventive and creative.
6. Each project must clearly illustrate which period was chosen.
7. You must provide me with your own evaluation criteria. This criteria must be turned in before you start the project, and you must turn in a graded copy when you turn in your final project.
8. If possible, turn in two copies so I can grade one and keep the other.

History and Analysis Midterm Project

Purpose: To do an in-depth study of a period of theatre

Choose one of the following:

1. Write a paper about an influential playwright or actor of a certain period in Theatre History. The paper must include the following:
   a. No more than one paragraph on the person's biographical information
   b. No more than two or three paragraphs on a summary of the crucial elements of this period in theatre
   c. Explain in detail why this person is influential to his or her time period
   d. Explain any influence or change this person has created for further drama periods (this requires in-depth critical analysis and research; don't skim the surface)
   e. Bibliography and footnotes or internal citations
   f. At least three different bibliography sources (Internet sources do not count)

2. Choose any play (one act or full length that you have not read before or during this class) and read it. Write an analysis paper consisting of the following:
   a. Not more than one paragraph summarizing the plot of the play
   b. Not more than two to three paragraphs explaining the drama period in which this play was written (be sure to include all crucial elements required for drama or that period)
   c. Explain in detail how this play did or did not meet the requirements of the period (address each element specifically as it pertains to the individual play)
   d. Not more than two paragraphs explaining why this play could or could not easily be performed in today's theatre
   e. Bibliography and footnotes or internal citations
   f. At least three different bibliography sources (the script book may be one source; Internet sources do not count)

You may choose a period not specifically studied in class.

Oscar Brockett's History of Theatre *is an excellent source for general information.*

Appendix B

Board-Approved Class Proposals*

*Passed in 1996, C.U.S.D. #185 Board of Education
Macomb, IL

Proposed Regular
or Eight-Block Drama Courses

by Raina Ames
Macomb Junior/Senior High School

CONTENTS

Computer-Aided Design in Theatre...53
Acting I...54
Introduction to Play Production..56
History and Analysis of Theatre...58

Course Description: Computer-Aided Design in Theatre

"Computer-Aided Design in Theatre," a tech prep, team-taught course that combines vocational technology with theatre, includes (1) the study of the computer-aided design program "3-D Studio"; (2) the refinement of design techniques with "3-D Studio"; (3) the study of theatrical set design; (4) the production of computer-generated set designs; and (5) the building of models or actual sets.

Course Goals

1. To learn, through lab exercises, the computer design program, "3-D Studio."
2. To explore, through drafting and representative models, the principal concepts behind theatrical set design.
3. To apply knowledge of both "3-D Studio" and theatrical set design by designing, drafting, and building set designs through models.
4. To solve basic introductory architecture problems through practice and experiment.
5. To construct actual representations of sets for Macomb High School play productions that are running concurrently. The express purpose will be to provide real-life applications of skills learned in design. (Students would design the sets that would be built.)
6. To provide opportunity to solve real-life application problems in computer design that will help build strong problem-solving skills.

Description of Appropriate Learners

"Computer-Aided Design in Theatre" is designed for upper-level students who will seek admission to colleges or universities in either architecture, theatrical design, or vocational education. This course will introduce students to computer-aided design (CAD) and theatrical set design; this class will give students a solid foundational knowledge that will better prepare them for a university program.

Requested Materials*

"3-D Studio" computer licenses and computer terminals
Theatrical set design textbook (optional)
White board for model building (could be a student cost)

Suggested Units

Unit I	Introduction to CAD—"3-D Studio" and practice	5 weeks
Unit II	Introduction and Analysis: Theatrical Design	3 weeks
Unit III	Design and Manual Drafting	3 weeks
Unit IV	CAD and Model Production	7 weeks

---

*The class size is structured around how many computer licenses are used. The ideal would be twenty students with twenty licenses, but the class could be structured so that half the class is using the computers while the other half was drafting manually (10/10 *as long as the course is team-taught*). It is a common complaint of college vocational technology professors that students do not have sufficient knowledge in manual drafting.

Rationale

In "Computer-Aided Design in Theatre," students would learn the basics of theatrical design and use 3-D Studio CAD along with manual drafting techniques to create original scene designs. These designs would be used for practical purposes in either the high school or junior high plays. Students would then help build these designs. Not only would students be getting design experience, they also would be getting practical knowledge and experience in watching designs they created being built for use in real-life situations.

The extracurricular programs would also benefit from this. Right now, there is not a strong technical crew built up for high school theatre productions. With students in this class being brought into the extracurricular process, the technical crew would not only receive much deserved recognition, but the level of ownership felt by high school students would dramatically increase; this increase would then further strengthen the pride put into *all* areas of theatre production.

Another gain would be in the wide knowledge base a student would take with him or her if planning an engineering or factory career after high school. In talking with Dr. Thomas Bridge, Chairman of the Vocational and Industrial Technology Department at Western Illinois University, what high school graduates entering his program seem to be lacking are basic skills in manual and computer drafting. By taking a practical subject such as theatre design for extra-curricular plays and combining it with computer design, the students leaving Macomb High School will have an advanced understanding of what is expected in their chosen field of CAD. At Western Illinois University, and I am sure at other universities as well, students who have not had basic training in CAD during high school are not recommended to enroll in the advanced engineering program that better prepares them for high-powered engineering jobs.

The most important gain for our district, however, would be that this class not only would easily lend itself to eight-block scheduling, but it would also fulfill a need for more Tech Prep classes in our school. This *team-taught, product-oriented* class covers engineering, theatre design, theatre analysis, computer graphics, and drafting. Further, the skills learned in this class are building blocks for anyone entering the field of theatre, engineering, industrial technology, or graphic arts. This could very easily lend itself to eventually being expanded to an advanced class that could become a pioneer in Illinois schools for preparing our computer and industrial technology students.

COURSE DESCRIPTION: ACTING I

"Acting I" is a theatre performance course that includes the (1) study of improvisational techniques; (2) step-by-step constructing of character analysis; (3) identification and application of appropriate acting techniques; (4) building of concentration and acting skills through monologue and group performance; and (5) exploring and creating of makeup and costume plots to help build a "whole" character.

Course Goals

1. To learn basic concepts of improvisation.
2. To explore characterization and setting significance through directed improvisational exercises.

3. To analyze acting characters by using learned character analysis techniques.
4. To analyze and create realistic characters through practice and performance of monologues.
5. To create realistic relationships between characters through practice and performance or dramatic and comedic scenes.
6. To reinforce performance confidence through production of group lip syncs.
7. To explore the use of costuming and makeup in theatre to help create a believable character.

Description of Appropriate Learners

"Acting I" is a performance course for students in grades 9–12 who are interested in exploring and enhancing knowledge and application of acting performance techniques.

Materials Needed

> Monologue and scene books
> Suggested books: *Monologues for Young Actors, Encore, 100 Movie Monologues, Scenes for Young Actors*
> Makeup (can be provided by students)
> Fellheimer Auditorium

SUGGESTED UNITS

Unit I	Introduction to Improvisation	2 weeks
Unit II	Introduction to Character Analysis	1 week
Unit III	Group Lip Syncs	2 weeks
Unit IV	Monologue Performance	6 weeks*
Unit V	Duet Scene Performance	5 weeks**
Unit VI	Final duet/monologue practice/performance	2 weeks

Rationale

In "Acting I," students would practice and hone improvisational, monologue and duet acting, and character analysis techniques. Students would also learn through practical application the importance of using stage makeup to create a character. All of these skills would be used to further the growth of student actors at Macomb High School. This in turn would help strengthen the extracurricular theatre program in the school. Fifteen years ago, students were challenged with all genres of theatre literature. Students performed *The Birds*, a Greek play; *Spoon River Anthology*, Reader's Theatre; *You Can't Take It with You*, lighthearted but challenging comedy; *The Tiger*, serious modern drama. Theatre classes that were in the curriculum regularly put together scenes for Arts Week and performed during the school day for peers. In short, the theatre program has lost a lot of the strength Maxine Joyce worked so hard to build. By bringing back performance classes, we can help reshape the theatre extracurricular program and bring back some of the pride once felt in its success.

---

*three monologues
**three scenes*

Another benefit is the immeasurable yet undeniable building of self-esteem that performance classes offer to students. In today's world, we cannot deny that teachers and schools have the responsibility of dealing with student problems that were unheard of years ago. Acting classes can give students a positive outlet in which to focus their energy. Students can work, learn, and grow not only as actors but as people as well. Aristotle said, "Acting is the study of Man in motion." By studying characters and defining why they behave as they do, students can identify with and ventilate emotions they may have in common with the characters they are portraying. There is a psychology to figuring out why characters do and say things; as actors, then, students can make value judgments as to the rightness and wrongness of those actions. This awareness of behavior inevitably causes a maturing in those involved in the process.

The biggest benefit, however, is the experience students will have in the arts. Right now, the state is mandating that schools prepare for fine arts assessment. The only arts classes offered at Macomb High School are visual art, music, and graphic arts; this does not reach the entire school population. Several students have expressed interest in being in plays, but they sometimes feel that the audition process is too overwhelming. A class in acting would take off some of the pressure because the audiences for their performances would be smaller; therefore, we can reach a wider body of students who have curiosities about theatre but do not want to commit to the big extracurricular productions. In addition, we have the thespians who are hungry for classes in theatre to improve their knowledge and ability in acting. Not every thespian gets cast in every show; five-week blocks are not enough time to concentrate on techniques for acting. By having a class in which thespians *and* inexperienced but interested students can get together and learn more about theatre, we drastically increase the number of students who are exposed to the fine arts. This then increases the level of success our students and our school will experience on the fine arts assessment tests.

COURSE DESCRIPTION: INTRODUCTION TO PLAY PRODUCTION

"Introduction to Play Production" is a course that includes (1) the study of basic principles in set construction, lighting design, costuming, acting, directing, and stage managing; (2) the refinement of directing and acting skills; (3) the construction of basic play scenery; and (4) the creation of working lighting designs for theatre.

Course Goals

1. To learn, through lab exercise and discussion, the basic elements of play production.
2. To explore, through hands-on experience, the principle concepts of directing.
3. To refine acting skills through practice and specific instruction.
4. To construct basic play scenery using knowledge of proper criteria.
5. To design costume plots using knowledge learned of costuming principles.
6. To demonstrate understanding of directing principles through practical application and production of scenes.

Description of Appropriate Learners

"Introduction to Play Production" is designed for students in grades 10–12 who are interested in exploring and strengthening their knowledge base in all aspects of theatre production.

Materials Needed

Play production textbook (recommended text: *Play Production Today*, fifth edition,
    Jonniepat Mobley)
1 × 4 × 16 wood*
Muslin*
Hardware tools*
Lighting equipment*
Macomb High School Drama Department costume access
Fellheimer Auditorium and scene shop

Suggested Units

Unit I	Introduction to Set Construction	3 weeks
Unit II	Introduction to Lighting Design	2 weeks
Unit III	Introduction to Costuming / Stage Makeup	2 weeks
Unit IV	Introduction to Stage Managing	2 weeks
Unit V	Introduction to Acting	3 weeks
Unit VI	Introduction to Directing	3 weeks
Unit VII	Play Production using Units I–VI to provide real-life application (possible public performance for elementary, junior high, or study halls)	3 weeks

Rationale

In "Introduction to Play Production," students would receive an overview of all the elements involved in play production. Through the study of set construction, lighting design, costuming and makeup, stage managing, acting, and directing, the students would be able to have a more in-depth study of play production than only working on extracurricular play productions could provide. Students would receive structured lecture and hands-on practice with the culminating project being a real-life application of all techniques learned by performing a production for elementary, junior high, or study hall students. This experience will necessitate the correct use of skills learned as well as provide a sense of accomplishment in all who participate.

    Another benefit is the strengthening of the extracurricular program. Until 1986, this very class was one of two theatre classes offered at Macomb High School. Having taken both of those classes myself, I can testify that, because I was given the chance to direct and act in this class, my self-confidence and sense of accomplishment drastically increased. I am not alone in this. Students who might not have otherwise tried out for extracurricular plays took this class because it was less threatening; however, through this class many people were recruited for work in the extracurricular program. Because students were spending time in class learning the basics of play production, students were much more capable of putting together smoother more professional extracurricular performances.

---

*Some materials can be provided or bought by the Macomb High School Drama Department—provided anything produced remains the property of the department with the intention for use in upcoming play productions; or one set of materials could be bought for the first class, then the only expense by the district each year would be new muslin, glue, and paint.

Yet another benefit is how performance classes easily lend themselves to fitting into eight-block scheduling. More time each day for every-other-day working on rehearsals and building is far more productive than meeting five days per week for less time. Students would show a greater amount of productivity getting one hour's work done in one longer class period than getting started and having to quit forty minutes later to clean up.

The biggest benefit, however, is the experience the students will have in the arts. Not only will this class reach those who take it, but the students who act as audiences for final projects will also be exposed to theatre as a fine art. Right now the state is mandating that schools prepare for fine arts assessment. The only arts classes offered at Macomb High School are visual art, music, and graphic arts. These classes do not reach the entire population of students at Macomb High School. If we were to have classes in theatre, we could reach a wider population of students. By having a class where students receive an overview of theatre, we drastically increase the number of students who are exposed to the fine arts. This then increases the level of success our students and our school will experience on the fine arts assessment tests mandated by the state.

COURSE DESCRIPTION: HISTORY AND ANALYSIS OF THEATRE

"History and Analysis of Theatre" is a course that includes (1) the study of historical trends in theatre; (2) the analysis of dramatic structure in dramatic literature; (3) the identification and evaluation of theme and symbolism in dramatic literature; and (4) the application of play analysis knowledge through evaluation of original playwriting works.

Course Goals

1. To learn significant trends in theatre history.
2. To identify specific influences theatre has on society and vice versa.
3. To analyze the structure of a play.
4. To identify and evaluate theme and symbolism in theatre by reading representative works from Greek to modern drama.
5. To create original play scripts which conform to learned conventions of theatre.
6. To analyze and evaluate original play scripts using learned analytical techniques.
7. To reinforce knowledge learned in history classes by analyzing the historical and social influences that affected the trends in theatre.

Description of Appropriate Learners

"History and Analysis of Theatre" is a course for upper-level students who are interested in theatre but want a nonperformance outlet for their interests.

Materials Needed

History of Theatre, Oscar Brockett
Assorted plays for analysis
An Introduction to Theatre and Drama, Marshall and Pat Cassady, eds.

Suggested Units

Unit I*	Egyptian/Greek/Roman Theatre	2 weeks
Unit II*	Medieval Theatre (Dark Ages)	1 week
Unit III*	Renaissance Theatre	2 weeks
Unit IV*	Restoration Theatre	1 week
Unit V*	Twentieth-Century Alternative Theatre	1 week
Unit VI*	Realism	3 weeks
Unit VII*	Modern Drama	2 weeks
Unit VIII	Playwriting and Self-Analysis	7 weeks

Rationale

In "History and Analysis of Theatre," students would receive an in-depth study of theatre history and play analysis along with a strengthening of understanding in the basic literature elements of dramatic structure, theme, and symbolism. Students would also get to experience play analysis through the creative process of original playwriting. Students would receive structured lecture and hands-on practice with the culminating project. This project would be a real-life application of all analysis and history elements learned by choosing a period in theatre history and writing a play that fits the historical and analytical requirements. This experience will encourage the correct use of skills learned and provide a sense of accomplishment in all who participate. Further, if there were to be an Acting or Introduction to Play Production class, the scripts generated in this class could possibly be used for performance in other classes.

Another benefit is the strengthening of the extracurricular program. For many years until 1986, this course was one of two theatre classes offered at Macomb High School. Having taken the play analysis class offered when I was in school, I was better prepared to go to college and use the knowledge learned in high school. I was better equipped to understand literature analysis, and I, like many other students from Macomb High School, could attribute my success to the fact that I had received in-depth training in high school.

The biggest benefit, however, is the experience the students will have in the arts. Right now, the state is mandating that schools prepare for fine arts assessments. The only arts classes offered at Macomb High School are visual art, music, and graphic arts. These classes do not reach the entire population of students at Macomb High School. Classes in theatre history, more than any other, would reach a wider population of students and more prepare them for an assessment test in the fine arts. By having a class in which students receive an overview of theatre history and analysis, we drastically increase the number of students who are exposed to the fine arts. This then increases the level of success our students and our school will experience on the fine arts assessment tests mandate by the state.

---

*Suggested integration of analysis and history of theatre by reading and analyzing plays during each unit of history.

Appendix C
Sample Schedules

The Diary of Anne Frank

We only have twenty-eight regular rehearsal days firmly set before tech rehearsals. Because of auditorium scheduling, we had to move the play up two weeks. I remind you of your signing of the clause that you will be at every rehearsal possible.

If you marked that an activity is flexible, I'll expect that you will come to rehearsals if they happen to conflict.

In addition, as was already clarified in the statement of commitment signed by you, we may have to have extra rehearsals if there are problems. In that case, you will get a few days' notice.

You also need to put in at least ten hours of set work, so you'll need to plan that. This set is going to be your home. I hope that you will take ownership of it. I'm going to ask that the cast contribute to the decoration of the set.

If you feel you need more rehearsal, I'll always be glad to schedule times with you.

2/11	6–9	Block Act I	
2/16	6–9	Block Act I	
2/17	6:15–9:15	Block Act II	
2/18	6–9	Act I	
2/19	3:15–6:15	Act II	
2/22	3–6	Act (short) {has to be at this time because of Pops Concert}	
2/23	6–9	Act (long)	
2/24	6:15–9:15	Act I	*OFF BOOK*
2/25	6–9	Act II	*OFF BOOK*
2/26	3:15–6:15	All	
3/1	6:15–9:15	All	STOP AND GO
3/2	6–9	Act I	
3/3	6:15–9:15	Act II	
3/4	6–9	All	
3/5	3:15–6:15	Problem Scenes	
3/8	6:15–9:15	All stop and go	
3/9	3:15–6:45	All stop and go	
3/10	6:15–9:15	Act I	
3/11	6–9	Act II	
3/12	3:15–6:15	All	
3/13–3/21	9–5	Definite set construction	
		Possible play rehearsals depending on shape of show	
3/22	6:15–9:15	Act I	
3/23	6–9	Act II	
3/24	6:15–9:15	Run (with props from now on)	

ALL THAT FOLLOW ARE MANDATORY REHEARSALS

3/25	6–10	Run (with sound from now on)
3/26	3–7	Run
3/29	3–6	Put up set if you can make it
	6:15–9:15	Run
3/30	6–9	Run
3/31	3:15–6:15	Run
4/1	1–4	Run
4/2		Possible rehearsal (if the show is awesome, no need to)
4/3		Possible rehearsal/possible dry tech
4/5	3–5	Makeup call
	5–Done	Run
4/6	3–5	Makeup call
	5–Done	Run
4/7	3–5	Makeup call
	5–Done	Run
4/8	9:05 a.m.	JH performance (must be there at least by first hour)
	5th–8th hour	Wear costumes for advertising
4/9	5:15	Makeup/tech call
	7:30	First performance
4/10	5:15	Makeup/tech call
	7:30	Second performance
4/11	12:15	Makeup/tech call
	2:30	Final performance
4/12	3–Done	Strike the set

GUYS AND DOLLS SONG GROUPS

GROUP A

Follow the Fold

FTF reprise

GROUP B

Fugue for Tinhorns

Guys and Dolls

GROUP C

Oldest Established

Luck Be a Lady

GROUP D

I'll Know

I've Never Been in Love Before

If I Were a Bell

GROUP E

Bushel and a Peck

Take Back Your Mink

Adelaide's Lament

A's reprise

GROUP F

More I Cannot Wish You

GROUP G

Sue Me

Marry the Man

GROUP H

Sit Down You're Rockin' the Boat

G and D reprise

GUYS AND DOLLS SCENE GROUPS

GROUP 1		GROUP 2		GROUP 3	
(11A)	1-1-1	(11B)	1-1-4	(11C)	1-1-6
(25A)	2-5-31	(11D)	1-1-8	(11I)	1-1-23
(25C)	2-5-38	(11E)	1-1-13	(12A)	1-2-24
(27A)	2-7-47	(11F)	1-1-15	(16A)	1-6-51
		(15A)	1-5-47	(22A)	2-2-7
		(11H)	1-1-19	(22B)	2-2-9
		(13A)	1-3-35	(25A)	2-5-31
		(15B)	1-5-47		
		(17A)	1-7-55		
		(11OB)	1-10-73		
		(23A)	2-3-11		
		(24A)	2-4-25		

GROUP 4		GROUP 5		GROUP 6	
(11G)	1-1-16	(12B)	1-2-26	(14B)	1-4-40
(14A)	1-4-38	(19A)	1-9-67	(14C)	1-4-45
(17B)	1-7-57	(110A)	1-10-70	(21C)	2-1-6
(21A)	2-1-1	(26A)	2-6-41	(24B)	2-4-28
(21B)	2-1-3				

GROUP 7	
(18A)	1-8-62

Key: Scripts labeled 1-1-1 = act-scene-page #. Combining act and scene (11) signals which part of the script. The letter represents a subsection of the scene as defined by director.

GUYS AND DOLLS REHEARSAL SCHEDULE*

*Subject to change with notice to actors

If you are only in selected parts of an act and wish to leave rehearsals, ask the director if you will be needed later in that rehearsal. If not, you are free to leave. *Please get permission first, however.*

	TIME	DANCING	SINGING	ACTING
M 1/31	6:15–9:30			READ THROUGH
T 2/1	6–9		6–7 GROUP H (All)	6–7 Adelaide
			7–7:30 GROUP A (Mission)	7–8:15 GROUP 2
			7:30–8:30 GROUP E (Hotbox)	
			8:15–9 Sky, Sarah, Arvide	
W 2/2	6:15–9:15		6:15–7:15 GROUP C (Men)	6:15–7:30 GROUP 3
			7:15–8:15 GROUP B	7:30–9:15 Group 5 + Havana
			8:15–8:45 GROUP F (Arvide)	
H 2/3	6–9	ASD	6–7 GROUP D (Sky/Sarah)	6–7:15 GROUP 6
			7–8 GROUP G (Nate, Ad, Sarah)	7:15–8 GROUP 4 minus AD
				8–9 GROUP 4 plus AD
F 2/4	3:15–6:15			3:15–6:15 GROUP 7
M 2/7	6:15–9:15		6–7 GROUP H (All)	
			7–8 GROUP D (Sky/Sarah)	7–8 GROUP 5
				8–9 GROUP 6
T 2/8	6–9		6–7 GROUP C (Men)	6–8 GROUP 1 (All)
			7–7:30 GROUP F (Arvide)	8–9 ALL (Crapshooters)
			7:30–8 Sarah	
W 2/9	6:15–9:15	6:15–6:45 Men	6:15–6:45 GROUP E (Hotbox)	6:15–9 Mission Band, Sarah, Sky, Arvide
		6:45–7:15 Havana	6:45–7:15 GROUP H	General Cartwright
		7:15–7:45 Men	7:15–7:45 ADELAIDE	
		7:45–8:15 Hotbox	7:45–8:15 GROUP	
		8:15–8:45 Havana	7:45–8:15 GROUP H	
		8:45–9:15 Hotbox		
H 2/10	6–9			6–9 RUN SHOW
F 2/11	3:15–6:15		3:15–4 GROUP B	
			4–4:30 GROUP G	
			4:30–5 GROUP D	
M 2/14	6:15–9:15			6:15–9:15 RUN ACT I
T 2/15	6–9			6–9 RUN ACT II
W 2/16	6:15–9:15	6:15–6:45 Men	6:15–6:45 GROUP A	6:15–9:15 GROUP 4
		6:45–7:15 Hotbox	6:45–7:15 GROUP C	
		7:15–7:45 Men	7:15–7:45 GROUP E	
		7:45–8:15 Havana	7:45–8:15 Nathan, Nicely, Benny	
		8:15–8:45 Hotbox		
		8:45–9:15 Havana		
H 2/17	6–9		6–7 GROUP E	6–8 GROUP 7
			7–8 Nathan/Adelaide	8–9 Sky and Sarah

	TIME	DANCING	SINGING	ACTING
F 2/18	3:15–6			3:15–6 GROUP 3
S 2/19	9–5	SET CONSTRUCTION/COSTUME ORGANIZATION		
M 2/21	1–4			1–2:30 GROUP 6
				2:30–4 GROUP 5
T 2/22	6–9			WORK ACT I
W 2/23	6:15–9:15	6:15–6:45 Men		WORK ACT II
		6:45–7:15 Hotbox		
		7:15–7:45 Havana		
		7:45–8:15 Hotbox		
		8:15–8:45 Men		
		8:45–9:15 Havana		
H 2/24	6–9			6–8 GROUP 1 (All)
				8–9 GROUP 2
F 2/25	3:15–5:30			3:15–5:30 GROUP 4
S 2/26	9–5	SET CONSTRUCTION		
M 2/28	3:15–5 (Pops Concert)		3:15–5 Run Act I *off book*	
T 2/29	6–9			6–9 Run Act II *off book*
W 3/1	6:15–9:15	6:15–6:45 Men		6:15–8:15 GROUP 2
		6:45–7:15 Hotbox		8:15–9:15 GROUP 3
		7:15–7:45 Havana		
		7:45–8:15 Hotbox		
		8:15–8:45 Men		
		8:45–9:15 Havana		
H 3/2	6–9			6–9 WORK ACT I
F 3/3	3:15–6:15			3:15–6:15 WORK ACT II
S 3/4 – 3/9	9–5	SPRING BREAK SET CONSTRUCTION		
M 3/13	4–7			4–6 GROUP 1
				6–7 GROUP 4
T 3/14	6–9			6–9 WORK ACT I
W 3/15	6:15–9:15	6:15–6:45 Men		6:15–9:15 WORK ACT II
		6:45–7:15 Hotbox	6:45–7:15 GROUP H	
		7:15–7:45 Havana	7:45–8:15 GROUP H	
		7:45–8:15 Hotbox		
		8:15–8:45 Men		
		8:45–9:15 Havana		
H 3/16	6–9			6–9 RUN SHOW
F 3/17	3–6			3–5 GROUP 2
				5–6 GROUP 6
S 3/18	9–5	SET CONSTRUCTION		
M 3/20	6:15–9:15			6:15–9:15 WORK ACT II
T 3/21	6–9			6–9 WORK ACT II

	TIME	DANCING	SINGING	ACTING
W 3/22	6:15–9:15	6:15–6:45 Hotbox		6:15–9:15 WORK ACT I
		6:45–7:15 Havana		
		7:15–7:45 Men		
		7:45–8:15 Hotbox		
H 3/23	3–6			3–6 WORK ACT II
F 3/24	1:30–5			1:30–5 Nathan, Nicely, Sky, Benny, Rusty, Sarah, Adelaide
S 3/25	9–5	SET CONSTRUCTION		
M 3/27	6:15–9:15			6:15–9:15 WORK ACT I
T 3/28	6–9			6–9 WORK ACT II
W 3/29	6:15–9:15			6:15–9:15 WORK ACT II
H 3/30	6–9			6–9 WORK ACT I
F 3/31	3:15–6:15			3:15–6:15 Sky/Sarah and Nate/Ad
S 4/1	8–12	SET CONSTRUCTION		
M 4/3	6:15–9:15			WORK ACT I
T 4/4	6–9			WORK ACT II
W 4/5	6:15–9:15			WORK ACT I
H 4/6	6–9			WORK ACT II
F 4/7	3:15–6:15			RUN SHOW
S 4/8	9–5	SET CONSTRUCTION		
M 4/10	6:15–9:15			RUN SHOW
T 4/11	6–9			RUN SHOW
W 4/12	6:15–9:15			RUN SHOW
H 4/13	6–9			RUN SHOW

MANDATORY REHEARSALS BEGIN NOW: ALL CAST REHEARSAL

	TIME	DANCING	SINGING	ACTING
F 4/14	3–6			RUN SHOW
S 4/15	9–5	SET CONSTRUCTION		
M 4/17	3–8		RUN SHOW; add lights/set change	
T 4/18	3–8		RUN SHOW add costumes	
W 4/19	3–DONE		RUN SHOW add all elements	
H 4/20	3–DONE		RUN SHOW WITH ALL ELEMENTS	
F 4/21	3–6		RUN SHOW no costumes	
M 4/24	3–DONE		FULL TECH	
T 4/25	3–DONE		FULL TECH	
W 4/26	3–DONE		FULL TECH	
H 4/27	3–DONE		LAST TECH (7 p.m. preview?)	
F 4/ 28	CALL TIMES: TBA		7:30 PERFORMANCE	
S 4/29	CALL TIMES: TBA		7:30 PERFORMANCE	
SU 4/30	CALL TIMES: TBA		2:30 PERFORMANCE	
M 5/1	3–DONE		STRIKE SETS/COSTUMES	

Guys and Dolls Scene Breakdown

(Highlight the scenes in which your character appears)

11A: Opening (1-1-1)

Bobbie Soxers
Sightseeing guide (Rusty Charlie)
Sightseers
Brannigan
Police officers
Well-dressed streetwalkers
Chorus girls: Carie Cook, Hillary Erdmann, Jessica Kuras, Lauren Rockwell,
     Heather Strohschein
Hurried Man/Benny Southstreet
Elderly woman street vendor
Sightseeing Texan
Texan's wife
Sidewalk photog
Elegant actresses
Actress' acquaintance (Harry the Horse)
Actor
A paper doll vendor
Heavyweight prizefighter
Manager
"Blind," drunk pickpocket
Passing male (also in 2-6-41)/Society Max
Nicely Nicely Johnson
Benny Southstreet
Rusty Charlie
Arvide Abernathy
Mission band
Joey Biltmore

11B: Fugue for Tinhorns (1-1-4)

Nicely
Benny
Rusty Charlie
Drunk
Joey Biltmore
Society Max
Harry the Horse
Streetwalkers

11C: Mission Band Entrance (1-1-6)

Mission band
Sarah
Arvide
Nicely
Benny
Rusty Charlie
Two Bobby soxers
ALL sightseers, prizefighter and manager, Opening chorus girls, Streetwalkers

11D: First Appearance (1-1-8)

Nicely	Harry the Horse
Benny	Josh Montalvo
Rusty Charlie	Craig Johnson
Brannigan	Two police officers
Nathan Detroit	Josh Balk
Zach Bartz	Martin McGee

11E: Oldest Established (1-1-13)

Nathan	Harry the Horse
Nicely	Benny
Rusty Charlie	ALL crapshooters MINUS Big Jule
Brannigan	Police officers
Adelaide	

Chorus Girls: Angie Balsamo, Katie Caldwell, Laura Combs, Amanda Wallen

11F: Don't Get Nathan in Trouble Scene (1-1-15)

Nathan	Harry the Horse
Nicely	Benny
Rusty Charlie	Adelaide

Chorus girls: Angie Balsamo, Katie Caldwell, Laura Combs, Amanda Wallen

11G: Adelaide Anniversary Scene (1-1-16)

Nathan	Adelaide
Benny	Nicely

Chorus girls: Angie Balsamo, Katie Caldwell, Laura Combs, Amanda Wallen

11H: Sky Cheesecake Scene (1-1-19)

Nathan	Sky
Benny	Nicely

11I: Sky Bets on Sarah (1-1-23)

Nathan   Sky
Benny   Nicely
Mission band   Sarah
Adelaide   Arvide
Bobby soxers   Elderly vendor woman

12A: Mission Scene (1-2-24)

Sarah   Arvide
Sky   Agatha
Calvin   Martha
Naomi

12B: Sky/Sarah (1-2-26)

Sky   Sarah

13A: Nathan on the Phone (1-3-35)

Nathan   Joey Biltmore

14A: Bushel and a Peck (1-4-38)

Master of ceremonies   Hotbox girls
Adelaide   Patrons
Waitresses/waiters

14B: Nathan Pie Face (1-4-40)

Nathan   Adelaide
Mimi   Hotbox girls
Patrons   Master of ceremonies

14C: Adelaide's Lament (1-4-45)

Adelaide

15A: Mission Band Follow the Fold (1-5-47)

Sarah   Mission Band
Arvide   Sky
Nicely   Benny

15B: Benny/Nicely (1-5-47)

Benny   Nicely
A doll: Heather Strohschein
A guy: Martin McGee

16A: The General's Ultimatum (1-6-51)

Sarah	Arvide
Mission band	General Cartwright
Sky	

17A: Big Jule (1-7-55)

Benny	Harry the Horse
Nathan	Nicely
Big Jule	Big Jule's girlfriend
The crapshooters	

17B: The Announcement of the Wedding (1-7-57)

Brannigan	Police officers
Adelaide	Benny
Harry the Horse	Nathan
Nicely	Big Jule
Big Jule's girlfriend	The crapshooters
Arvide	Mission band

18A: HAVANA (1-8-62)

Havana dancers	Fashionable dancers
Head waiter	Other waiters and waitresses
Sarah	Sky

19A: If I Were a Bell (1-9-67)

Sky	Sarah

110A: My Time of Day/I've Never Been in Love Before (1-10-73)

Sky	Sarah
Arvide	Mission band
ALL crapshooters	Joey Biltmore
Brannigan	Police officers

21A: Take Back Your Mink (2-1-1)

Master of ceremonies	Hotbox girls
Adelaide	Patrons
Waiters/waitresses	

21B: Sky/Nathan/Adelaide (2-1-3)

Waiter	Sky
Nicely	Adelaide

21C: Adelaide's Lament reprise (2-1-6)

Adelaide

22A: More I Cannot Wish You (2-2-7)

Sarah   Arvide

22B: Where's the Crap Game? (2-2-9)

Sarah   Arvide
Nicely   Sky

23A: Big Jule Takes over the Sewer/Luck Be a Lady (2-3-11)

Harry the Horse   Big Jule
Big Jule's girlfriend   Player
Another player   Nathan
Benny   Nicely
Sky   ALL crapshooters

24A: The Wrath of Adelaide (2-4-25)

ALL crapshooters   Big Jule
Big Jule's girlfriend   Harry
Nathan   Adelaide
Benny   Nicely

24B: Sue Me (2-4-28)

Nathan   Adelaide

25A: Bringing Them into the Fold (2-5-31)

Mission band   General Cartwright
Arvide   Sarah
Sky   ALL crapshooters
Hotbox girls   Big Jule
Big Jule's girlfriend   Benny
Nathan   Harry
Brannigan   Police officers

25B: Sit Down You're Rockin' the Boat (2-5-35)

ALL

25C: Brannigan (2-5-38)

ALL

26A: Marry the Man (2-6-41)

Sarah   Adelaide

27A: Guys and Dolls reprise (2-7-47)

ALL

Appendix D
Sample Audition Form

_____ Put an X on the line if you *do not* wish to be considered for individual roles (Leads, Hotbox Girls, Rusty, and Benny)

Name _____

Phone # _____

Height _____

Year in school _____

Extracurricular/Work Schedules

(Anything *not* flexible may inhibit casting in a lead role. Anything you do not list may either cause you to be replaced, or you will have to rearrange that unlisted schedule so it does not interfere with musical rehearsal schedule.)

	Activity Name	Specific Time	Flexible (yes or no)
Monday			
Tuesday			
Wednesday			
Thursday			
Friday			
Saturday			
Sunday			

Women: Do you have character shoes?   Yes _____   No _____

Do you have tap shoes?   Yes _____   No _____

All: What, if any, musical instruments do you play? (list all)

If not cast, would you be willing to work on a crew? Yes _____ No _____

GUYS and DOLLS ACTOR CONTRACT:

Please read the following and then sign in the space provided. Make sure you read this carefully. This is a binding agreement between you and directors:

By signing, you are stating that you understand that just because you audition for one part does not mean the directors are obligated to give you that part. The directors will place you wherever they think you most fit the character and the needs of the directors. You understand that being in the chorus is a big time commitment, but you also know that the lead roles (Sarah, Adelaide, Hotbox Girls, Sky, Nathan, Nicely Nicely, Arvide, Rusty, and Benny, and the Salvation Army band) will require extra rehearsal time. The more lines or songs you have, the bigger your time commitment will be. You understand that you are allowed two (2) absences from rehearsals before the directors have the right to remove you from a scene or replace you all together. Dancers will have to be available Wednesday nights from six until nine o'clock in the evening to work with the choreographer, but the Hotbox Girls and the Crapshooters will have to come to the rehearsals on other days when these scenes and songs are being worked.

In addition, everyone is expected to be in attendance the last ten rehearsals before we open—with no excuses and no questions asked. It takes a lot of work to get a musical ready to perform. You must commit to making this as successful as possible. Each cast member is asked to put in at least ten hours of work on either the set construction or costume coordination, and any extra time you could give would be very much appreciated.

If you wish to be considered for a leading role, you have to understand the time commitment involved. We are asking that anyone cast in a lead rearrange his or her outside schedule to fit musical rehearsals. We will schedule around conflicts as much as possible, but if you are a lead and rehearsal is scheduled during another activity you have, you will have to make the musical the priority. For instance, after solo and ensemble contest is over, you will be asked to rearrange lesson schedules so that you can make it to rehearsals. You absolutely can't come and go to different activities if you are a lead. If we get into that, you will be replaced. If you are not willing or able to make these schedule accommodations, *please do not put yourself up for lead roles.*

All company members are expected to be at every scheduled rehearsal. If you have unexcused absences from rehearsal, you can either be replaced in a number or acting scene, or you may be asked to leave the cast altogether. If you need to go for a doctor's appointment or if you are absent from school, please get word to either Ms. Ames or the stage manager *before* rehearsal begins. If you have many absences, whether excused or unexcused, that interfere with the running of a scene, you may be replaced with others who don't have as many conflicts.

In terms of sports conflicts, if you are in swimming, you will need to make some compromises the first three weeks of musical rehearsal. You may have to leave swim practice early to get to musical practice at a certain time. If you are in track, according to the coach, you cannot be in the play at all. If you are in softball or baseball, you cannot be considered for anything more than chorus because your games take you out of school and thus rehearsal time far too many days in any given week. Any other sports you are concerned about need to be talked about with the directors before we cast the show. Any athlete who also wants to be in the musical needs to understand that you have to be at rehearsals when they are scheduled. This means that if you are finished at the sports practice at six o'clock in the evening and have to be at musical rehearsal at the same time, you can't take your time getting there. You may have parents or friends deliver food to you, but you can't drive off and take your time in between these. Therefore, be absolutely sure you want to do both of those activities.

Finally, if you don't get cast in a role that you wanted and you think you will be miserable in the smaller role, please come and talk to us. I would have much more respect you for bowing out of the show instead of staying in and causing trouble with a negative attitude. There are so many good actors and singers, but only one person can be chosen for any given role. We are looking for specific types of performers who have to be able to do certain combinations of things for each of the parts. This does not mean that you are worse than someone else if you don't get cast in a lead. It just might mean you are committed to activities that conflict with rehearsal schedules. It is okay if you make other things your priority, but you have to understand that to put together a quality show, we are going to assemble together those who are most willing or able to make the musical their number one commitment.

_____

(Student signature)

Appendix E
Class Assignments, Activities, and Lesson Plan Ideas

Scene Design

PROJECT REQUIREMENTS:

1. Choose a play you would like to read.
2. Choose one setting from this play. (If it only has one setting, your choice has already been made.) This one setting is the subject of your design.
3. Do a survey of your auditorium space. Use the *Stage & School* text checklist criteria. Include all parts as well as measurements of stage dimensions, wing space, curtain areas, house seat proportions, and sight lines.
4. Discuss with me the show's concept so you have a basis from which to work on a set design.
5. Write a paragraph or two explaining what the director's concept is, character relationships, theme, focuses in the play (or scene), period, time of year, and function of the specific area you are designing. (I'm the director.)
6. Make a floor plan for the acting area.
7. Make a perspective 3-D drawing of what the set would look like from the audience. (If you are not an artist, do not despair. Just make sure everything is drawn the right size and in the right places. This grade is not going to be based on how good your drawing looks—do you meet all the criteria? That is your goal.)
8. Attach to the 3-D drawing swatches of color for the set so we get an idea of the color palette.
9. Write another few paragraphs justifying the choice of line, style, colors, placement of set pieces, and what elements of the set are used to show the period. (This is basically the written justification of what you have done with the design and why. Please don't leave anything out. Check your textbook, Chapter 10, to make sure you have covered everything.)
10. Put items one through eight together in a polished, presentational form and turn it in Tuesday, March 14. You will have time in class to do the questioning of the director and auditorium evaluation, but the bulk of this will be outside work.

UPCOMING SCHEDULE:

2/4	Auditorium survey
2/7–2/15	Duet acting work
2/9	Scores due (such as the monologue scores—for your character only)
2/10	Memorization check
2/16 and 2/17	Performances of duet acting scenes
2/18–3/17	Set construction (*wear clothes you can get dirty with paint, etc.*)
3/14	Scene designs due in class (you will informally present your design to the class this day)

NAME _____

Scenic Design Checklist

(Once you have completed this checklist, attach it to your final product)

_____ Chosen set design & play

_____ Auditorium space survey

_____ Paragraphs explaining the following:

      _____ director's concept

      _____ character relationships

      _____ theme

      _____ focuses

      _____ period

      _____ time of year

      _____ function of the specific design area

_____ Floor plan of acting area

_____ Perspective 3-D drawing of what the set should look like from audience

_____ Color swatches attached to the 3-D drawing

_____ A NEAT package of all

NAME _____

Scenic Design Rubric

Auditorium Space Survey

1	2	3	4	5
Not at all complete	Only some parts present, but incomplete	All parts present, but very sparse	All parts present; some areas sparse	All parts present and complete

Director's Concepts

1	3	5	7	10
Not at all detailed; does not match design	Lots of detail but is not at all carried through in design	*Bare bones,* but concept carried through to design	Very well explained, but some meaning lost in transfer to design *or* matched design well but not a firm explanation	Great explanation; great carry out in design

Character Relationships, Focus, and Function of Set

1	3	5	7	10
Not at all detailed; does not match design	Lots of detail, but is not at all carried through in design	*Bare bones,* but concept carried through to design	Very well explained, but some meaning lost in transfer to design *or* matched design well but not a firm explanation	Great explanation; great carry out in design

Theme, Period, Time of Year

1	3	5	7	10
Not at all detailed; does not match design or director's concept	Lots of detail, but is not at all carried through to design	*Bare bones,* but concept carried through to design	Very well explained, but some meaning lost in transfer to design *or* matched design well but not a firm explanation	Great explanation, justified; well executed in design

Floor Plan

5	10	15	17	20
Sloppy; little or no evidence of thought to needs of the play; not at all functional	Mostly sloppy; some evidence of thought to needs of the play; not very functional	Somewhat sloppy; much evidence of thought to needs of the play; somewhat functional	Mostly neat; much evidence to needs of the play: *mostly* evidence of thought to needs; function	Neat; well planned; much evidence of thought to the needs of the play; *very* functional

3-D Drawing

1	3	5	7	10
Sloppy; little or no evidence of thought to needs of the play; style/period nonexistent	Mostly sloppy; some evidence of thought to needs of the play; style/period off	Somewhat sloppy; much evidence of thought to needs of the play; loosely fits style/period	Mostly neat; much evidence to needs of the play; mostly fits style/period	Neat; well planned; much evidence to needs of the play; completely fits style/period

Colors

1	2	3	4	5
Not at all logical	Mostly poorly chosen	Somewhat logical choices	Mostly logical choices; mostly justified	Extremely logical; well chosen

Oral Presentation

1	3	5	7	10
Not at all defended	Defended only a little	Defended but holes in the explanation	Mostly well defended	Extremely well defended

TOTAL _____

Makeup Morgue
Project Requirements*

(Use pictures from magazines to get these parts of the body for reference. Choose ages you could really change yourself if using makeup. Have at least ten different cutouts for each section. The emphasis is on getting *different looks*—not all the same.)

1. Title page (with name, period, class name)
2. Eyes
3. Mouths: lips and teeth separate
4. Hair: female
5. Hair: male
6. Body types
7. Hands
8. Unrealistic/fantasy
9. Age
10. Accessories
11. Miscellaneous: wrinkles/folds/birth marks (special identifying features)
12. A final, chosen face that you will try to make yourself look like (study the size of lips, shadowing, size of nose, eyebrow placement, color of eyelids, etc.)

While others are practicing, you will get tutorials in makeup application and special makeup techniques.

Makeup Morgue Rubrics

1. (5) _____ Title page (with name, period, class name)
2. (5) _____ Eyes
3. (5) _____ Mouth: lips and teeth (ten pictures each)
4. (5) _____ Noses
5. (5) _____ Hair: female
6. (5) _____ Hair: male
7. (5) _____ Body types
8. (5) _____ Hands
9. (5) _____ Unrealistic/fantasy
10. (5) _____ Age
11. (5) _____ Accessories
12. (5) _____ Miscellaneous: wrinkles/folds/birth marks (special identifying features)
13. (5) _____ A final, chosen face that you will try to make yourself look like (study the size of lips, shadowing, size of nose, eyebrow placement, color of eyelids, etc.)

---

*Original idea for this assignment came from Lori Caldwell-Hopkins, McCutcheon High School, Lafayette, Indiana.

Makeup Due Dates

(Makeup and directing assignments to work consecutively)

Second-round directors have makeup application test due 4/24

Second-round directors have makeup morgues due 4/27

First-round directors have makeup application test due 5/8

First-round directors have makeup morgues due 5/11

Class Procedures for Directing/Makeup Phases:

First-round scenes:

   4/15: Audition and first read-through

   4/16, 4/17, 4/20, 4/21, 4/22, 4/23, 4/24: Rehearse scenes

   4/27: Performances of scenes

Second-round scenes:

   4/29: Audition and first read-through

   4/30, 5/1, 5/4, 5/5, 5/6, 5/7, 5/8: Rehearse scenes

   5/11: Performance of scenes

Director's Book/Directing Assignment

INSTRUCTIONS AND CHECKLISTS*

Assignment: Choose a one-act play and address all items listed. Everything must be typed and presented in a polished and professional manner. Use size 12 or 14 pt., standard type font. You will make an informal presentation of your scenic design on completion. Binders will be provided to you.

PART I—DIRECTOR'S BOOK

1. Name of play
2. Name of author
3. Name of director (you)
4. Statement of theme (universal lesson learned—a complete statement)
5. Statement of dramatic action (just for your scene; not the entire play):
   a. Exposition
   b. Inciting incident (introduction of conflict)
   c. Rising action (events that happen because of the conflict)
   d. Climax (point of no return; course of events are set in motion and cannot be reversed)
   e. Falling action (events that happen because of the climax)
   f. Resolution (the final outcome)
6. Locale (place where story takes place, as chosen by director)
7. Time of day; season
8. Play's range of emotions (cite them in order that they happen in the play)
9. Discussion of character (for every character in the scene):
   a. Superobjective (one overriding need)
   b. Distinguishing personality characteristics (cite "proof" from script)
   c. Relationship to others in the scene (family/friend/like/dislike/why?)
10. Floor plan of acting area (use diagonals to create more interesting blocking—may be a photocopy of your scenic design)
11. Actual script with the following:
    a. Entire script divided into beats (shifts in motivation)
    b. Each beat includes analysis of:
       i.   Overriding theme of the beat
       ii. Description of mood (use at least three adjectives to describe)
       iii. The objective or tactic each character takes
    c. List of blocking moves (stage directions)

PART II—DIRECTING SCENE

Assignment: Using the directing book to direct a scene for class.

1. Complete all components for the director's book.
2. Cast from study hall students
3. Rehearse
4. Present scene for the class

---

*Adapted from assignment created by egla birmingham, Western Illinois University, Macomb, IL.

Director's Book

GRADING RUBRIC

___ (5) Statement of theme

Statement of Dramatic Action

___ (2) Exposition

___ (2) Inciting incident (introduction of conflict)

___ (2) Rising action

___ (2) Climax

___ (2) Falling action/resolution

___ (2) Locale

___ (2) Time; season

___ (2) Play's range of emotions

Discussion of Character

___ (2) Superobjective (one overriding need)

___ (2) Distinguishing personality characteristics

___ (2) Relationship to others in the scene

___ (3) Floor plan of acting area (use diagonals to create more interesting blocking)

Actual Script with the Following:

___ (4) Whole script divided into beats

Each beat includes analysis of:

___ (4) Overriding theme of the beat

___ (4) Description of mood (use at least three adjectives to describe)

___ (4) The objective or tactic each character takes

___ (4) List of blocking moves

Director's Scene

GRADING RUBRIC

Blocking

(10) ___ Logical/workable

(10) ___ Motivated

CHARACTERIZATION

(10) ___ Motivation/intentions

(10) ___ Costuming/props

(5) ___ Mood

(5) ___ Floor plan

(10) ___ Pacing

DRAMATIC STRUCTURE

(5) ___ Opening clear/definite

(5) ___ Climax

(5) ___ Resolution

(5) ___ Conflict

Sample Director's Book for an Excerpt of
Much Ado About Nothing

PART I—DIRECTOR'S BOOK

1. Name of play: *Much Ado About Nothing*
2. Name of author: William Shakespeare
3. Name of director: Raina Ames
4. Statement of theme: True love survives in spite of the pride of women and men.
5. Statement of dramatic action:
   a. Exposition
      i.   Benedick, Don Pedro, Claudio, Don John return from war.
      ii. Hero, Beatrice, Leonato welcome them.
   b. Inciting incident (introduction of conflict)
      i.   Claudio declares interest in Hero, and Benedick is deceived into believing Beatrice loves him.
   c. Rising action
      i.   Claudio proposes marriage to Hero (through Don Pedro).
      ii.   Benedick convinces himself he is in love with Beatrice (his former girlfriend).
      iii. Beatrice is deceived into believing Benedick is sick with love for her.
      iv.   They flirt with the notion of getting back together.
      v.   Don John plots to make everyone miserable.
      vi.   Don John has his associate seduce Margaret at Hero's window.
      vii. Claudio sees seduction and gets enraged.
      viii. At the wedding, Hero is accused of being unfaithful to Claudio.
      ix.   Claudio disgraces Hero and storms out.
      x.   Leonato denounces his daughter.
      xi.   After Hero faints, Claudio and Don Pedro leave.
      xii. Beatrice demands that Benedick kill Claudio for this injury.
      xiii. The Friar decides Hero should pretend to be dead until the truth can be revealed.
      xiv. Claudio learns of Hero's death.
      xv.   Claudio goes to the grave to repent.
      xvi. Don John's dastardly deed is revealed.
      xvii. Claudio is made to marry Leonato's "niece" (Hero in disguise) as the only way to restore Hero's good name.
      xviii. Don John and his associates are exposed.
      xix. Claudio is let in on the secret about Hero.
      xx.   Benedick and Beatrice give in to their love.
      xxi. The rightful lovers end up together, and order is restored.
   d. Climax
      i.   The Friar decides Hero should pretend to be dead until the truth can be revealed.
   e. Falling action
      i.   Claudio learns of Hero's death.
      ii.   Claudio goes to the grave to repent.
      iii. Don John's dastardly deed is revealed.
      iv.   Claudio is made to marry Leonato's "niece" (Hero in disguise) as the only way to restore Hero's good name.

     v.   Don John and his associates are exposed.
     vi.   Claudio is let in on the secret about Hero.
     vii. Benedick and Beatrice give in to their love.
  f. Resolution
     i.   The rightful lovers end up together, and order is restored.

6. Locale: Sixteenth-century Italy

7. Time/season: Three days and nights in late spring

8. Play's range of emotions (cite them in order they happen in the play): Victorious celebration, infatuation, playful antagonism, passion, suspicion, naked rage, accusatory condemnation, righteous anger, regret, redemption, adulation.

9. Discussion of character: *Beatrice*
  a. Superobjective (one overriding need)
    To be respected and to protect herself in a man's world.
  b. Distinguishing personality characteristics (cite "proof" from script)
    Pride, intelligence, wit, stubbornness
  c. Relationship to others in the scene (family/friend/like/dislike/why?)
    With Benedick: they are former lovers; they have a playfully antagonistic relationship, but there is an underlying open wound from the breakup of their past relationship. Proof:
    "Against my will I am sent to bid you come to dinner"
    "I took no more pains for those thanks than
      you take pains to thank me. If it had been painful,
      I would not have come"
    "You have no stomach, signor?"

    (all other characters would be analyzed as well)

10. Floor plan of acting area (use diagonals to create more interesting blocking; may be a photocopy of your scenic design)

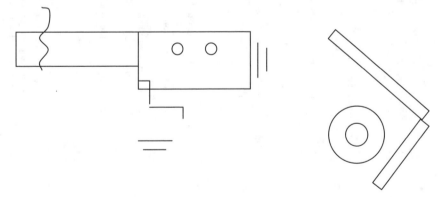

11. Actual script with the following:
  a. Entire script divided into beats (shifts in motivation)
  b. Each beat includes analysis of:
    i. Overriding theme of the beat
    ii. Description of mood (use at least three adjectives to describe)
    iii.The objective or tactic each character takes
  c. List of blocking moves (stage directions)

SEE NEXT PAGE

Theme: deciphering feelings Mood: perplexed, ambivalent, piqued Benedick: to reason, to weigh options	(1) *Exeunt Pedro, Claudio and Leonato.* Benedick: (*coming forward*) This can be no trick. The conference was sadly bourne. They have the truth of this from Hero. They seem to pity the lady. It seems her affections have their full bent. (2) Love me? Why, it must be requited. I hear how I am censured. They say I will bear myself proudly, if I perceive the love come from her; (3) they say too that she will rather die than give any sign of affection. I did never think to marry. I must not seem proud; happy are they that hear their detractions and can put them to mending. They say the lady is fair; (4) 'tis a truth, I can bear them witness; and virtuous, 'tis so, I cannot reprove it; and wise but for loving me; by my troth, it is not addition to her with, nor no great argument or her folly, for I will be terribly in love with her. (5) I may chance have some odd quirks and remnants of wit broken on me, because I have railed so long against marriage. But doth not the appetite alter? Shall quips and sentences and these paper bullets of the brain awe a man from the career of his humor?	(1) **They exit out #3 while Benedick crawls along and watches them go—gets on knees collapsing on round bench** (2) **stand—SR of round bench** (3) **USL of round bench** (4) **in a daze—tries to lean into shrub; hand gets pricked—rubs hand—sits on USL of round bench—swings legs into center and face DSR** (5) **sink into center of round bench**
Theme: declaration of love Mood: exalted, triumphant; spacious Benedick: to expose his love	(6) No, the world must be peopled! When I said I would die a bachelor; I did not think I should live till I were married. (7) Here comes Beatrice. By this day, she is a fair lady! *Enter Beatrice*	(6) **stands in center of round bench** (7) **struggles to get out as BEA enters #1**
Theme: cat and mouse Mood: snippy, quick, cagey Benedick: to feel her out Beatrice: to get the better of him	Beatrice: (8) Against my will I am sent to bid you come to dinner. Benedick: (9) Fair Beatrice, I thank you for your pains. Beatrice: I took no more pains for those thanks than you take pains to thank me. If it had been painful, I would not have come. (10) Benedick: You take pleasure in the message? Beatrice: Ye, just so much as you may take upon a knife's point. (11) You have no stomach, signor? Fare you well. (12) *Exits away from others*	(8) **she stops on platform at the stairs** (9) **X USR to stairs, foot up on one** (10) **turns to go—he is up on platform in front of her** (11) **she tries to get past; he blocks her** (12) **she goes down steps and out #4**
Theme: staking claims Mood: celebratory, reveling, honorable Benedick: to coax himself to love	Benedick: Ha! "Against my will I am sent to bid you come to dinner." There's a double meaning in that. "I took no more pains for those thanks than you took pains to thank me." That's as much to say, "Any pains that I take for you is as easy as thanks." If I do not pity her, I am a villain; If I do not lover her, I am a rascal. I will go get her picture. (13)	(13) **he follows her out #4**

Acting Lesson Ideas

Finding the Action in Scenes (to be used as an exercise while students are working on dialogues)

1. Warm-ups
   a. Stretch high
   b. Stretch side to side
   c. Stretch flat back
   d. Fall over
   e. Slowly roll up
   f. Head rolls side to side
   g. Repeat all
2. Walking in clumps (as yourself)
   a. Walk left
   b. Walk right
   c. About face
3. Discussion: What have you noticed?
4. Walk as your character
   a. Call out directions
   b. Ask students to pose as a statue (in character)
   c. Get them walking again
   d. Ask student to pose as a statue (four different poses total)
5. Get with your acting partner
   a. Walk in pairs in character
   b. Consider the relationship between the characters; how do you feel about the other person? How do you show it in this walk?
6. Interactive statue poses
   a. Think of your character's intentions
   b. Think of your objectives: what do you want to get from this other person?
   c. Create interactive statue poses (four total)
7. Discussion: Anything new you found about your relationships?

FOLLOW-UP:

1. Spread out
2. As teacher says a word, students repeat it and give it a physical action (keep action going and commit). *Words:* Is, be, show, tell, get him to see
3. Discussion: What's the problem with these words? (not active—can't physically communicate "be")
4. New words: attack, shame, inspire, rescue
5. Discussion: What's the difference?
6. Talk about ways you could "raise the stakes" like this in your scenes (Make sure you use *active* intentions)
7. Think through the first three beats of your scene. Give me the action verb that describes your character's intention
8. Discussion: *What have you learned?*

A/B SCENES

(Use as a way to help students create intention/motivation for characters and scenes)

Directions: Give students these scenes in pairs. Give them two minutes to discuss a place for this scene, but do not let them discuss each other's intentions. Direct students to keep these to themselves. Coach them to make bold, *active* choices. After all the scenes, discuss the differences and what moments were most clear, specific)

SCENE 1:

A: You told him.

B: Yes, I told him.

A: Isn't there something else we should do?

B: Maybe.

A: What do you think?

B: It's hard to say!

A: Don't you know?

B: What are you after?

A: It's hard to know.

B: You'll find out soon.

SCENE 2:

(This scene can be very helpful at playing the opposite and exploring connotation vs. denotation)

A: You look nice.

B: Thank you.

A: Yeah, you look really good.

B: Thank you very much.

Playwriting Ideas:
Teachers' Workshop Brainstorming

1. Modernize scenes from older plays
2. Video student acting of modernized plays
3. Costumes research projects tied in with plays; models of Globe Theatre, costume design, history of piece
4. Incorporate dialogue into writing
5. Write an original script
6. Show characterization through dialogue
7. Use literature as a springboard for an original scene
8. Use modern plays (what are the new classics? — *see* Appendix P)
9. Use same selection to examine different director/character interpretations
10. Have students perform their writing
11. Use solo, duet scenes to understand passages
12. Read short stories — get play ideas generated from these
13. Incorporate improvisations based on serious matters/current events
14. Make things more relative to them through latest movies seen; making parallels — what attracts them to story/issue?
15. Boiling down to an overall theme
16. Using variations on same theme: *10 Things I Hate About You, Lion King* to teach *Hamlet*
17. Improvisations to interpret literature (possibly *Beowulf*/Arthurian legends)
18. Translate dialogue of older works into their own words
19. Journaling: using these outcomes as seed ideas for original plays. "What is school pride to you?" and other topics that have relevance to the students

20. Appealing to their senses: testing how they will be opened up
    - Showing pictures/photos
    - Showing artwork
    - Showing colors
    - Exposing to smells
    - Playing music
    All to inspire students to write
21. Improv sections to short stories; get students seeing what they are reading to stimulate their imagination
22. Getting student active/tactile
23. Using tableau: five still scenes of short stories; students freeze in the tableau of an important scene from a story
24. Highlight elements of short stories and describing these as dramatic; showing the parallels between genres
25. Have students write their own ending; write one or more paragraph: "I would end it like this..."
26. Have student be as descriptive as possible: do an adjective exercise where students use as many adjectives in writing a monologue in order to paint as many pictures as possible
27. Have students focus on characterization: study characters in writing — use personality charts to pinpoint character elements
28. Use A/B scenes to get students on their feet and interacting to discover character intention
29. Have students dramatize moments in history both on their feet and in writing

Barter Theatre/Theatre Virginia Partnership, 9/26/02
Facilitated by Raina Ames

Lesson Plan Ideas

TABLEAU

(Detailed explanation of #23 from *Playwriting Ideas* on the previous page)

1. At the end of a short story unit, have groups of students do freeze frames of significant moments in short stories they have studied.
2. Have students guess which story is being represented.
3. Discuss the significance of the scenes represented and why they are important to the story.
4. You can adapt this to specifically represent elements of dramatic structure: exposition, inciting incident/narrative hook, rising action, climax, falling action, and resolution. It can be used as a tactile quiz for students, or it can be a form of review for a unit test.

IMPRESSIONIST ART DIALOGUE

1. Show several impressionist paintings to students.
2. Have students in groups of two pick a picture with at least two people in it.
3. Groups write dialogue based on nonverbal communication indicated in the painting.
4. Students act out dialogue for the class.
5. *Follow-up:* Discuss nonverbal communication and how we use it as either a completely different language or as a supplement to verbal communication.

Appendix F

Lecture Notes and Handouts

History and Analysis of Theatre Lecture Notes

The following are the theatre history notes I used in my class. If you have an opaque projector, you may use them just as they are, or you may wish to photocopy them onto transparencies.

THEATRE HISTORY IN A NUTSHELL

- Greek vs. Roman Theatre

- The Dark Ages and Medieval Drama

- The Renaissance

- Seventeenth- and Eighteenth-Century Transitional Drama

- Romanticism and Nineteenth- and Twentieth-Century Drama

- Realism

- Absurdist Theatre

- Alternative Theatre

- Musical Theatre

THE BEGINNINGS OF GREEK DRAMA

Egypt—had acrobatic dancers-rituals-storytelling; already saw people's nature for imitation to escape everyday life.

Greek Drama—1250 B.C. earliest recording of Festival

Festival of Dionysus (god of wine/fertility)

- Zeus/Semele—killed, dismembered, resurrected = fertility/revelry

- Started as a place of intoxication, orgy, devouring of human sacrifice

- This evolved to a *tragos* (goat sacrifice)

- Dithyrambs—hymns sung by 50 men led by a priest; these told episodes of Dionysus' life

- Thespis—first man to step forward and say lines

- Festival represents rebirth; guarantees spring's return

ARISTOTLE'S POETICS: THE FIRST RULES OF DRAMA

EVERY DRAMA NEEDS SIX PARTS:

1. Plot (beginning/middle/end; unified with a conflict)

2. Character (tragic hero and hubris {one tragic flaw})

3. Thought (characters need motivation)

4. Diction (connotation, inflection, poetic)

5. Music (songs with chorus, told exposition or narration)

6. Spectacle (deus ex machina {machine of the gods} and other devices)

• Audience must experience a purging of emotions and relate to the character.

THREE UNITIES were born: TIME (less than a day—real time)

ACTION (no subplots—one focus)

PLACE (doesn't change locale)

• Birth of Dramatic Structure

DRAMATIC STRUCTURE

GENESIS OF ALL THEATRE: CONFLICT

Man vs. man; man vs. self; man vs. nature; man vs. supernatural

DRAMATIC STRUCTURE

Exposition
(background information)

Inciting Incident
(introduction of conflict)

Rising Action
(events that complicate the problem)

Climax
(the highest point of action)

Denouement
(falling action)

Resolution
(final end to the conflict)

THIS ALL SET THE STANDARD FOR GREEK TRAGEDY

GREEK TRAGEDY

CHARACTERISTICS

1. Prologue (give information of events before beginning of story)

2. Parados (entrance of chorus, give exposition, establish mood)

3. Series of episodes (3–6)

    • Divided by choral songs (stasima)

    • These are supposed to develop the main actions

4. Exodus (concluding scene; departure of all characters)

5. Physical violence offstage (just tell about and show bodies at end)

6. Follow three unities

7. Based on myth or history *but* playwrights invent motivations of characters and events (psychological and ethical)

SOPHOCLES: OEDIPUS REX

- Increased emphasis on individual characters

- Reduced role of chorus

- Complex, well-motivated characters

- Protagonists noble but not faultless (deviates from hubris)

- Exposition carefully motivated

- Scenes are built through suspense to a climax

- Action clear, logical

- Poetry highly regarded

No elaborate visual effects (the impact is from the force of the dramatic action; don't need "tricks")

AMPHITHEATRES

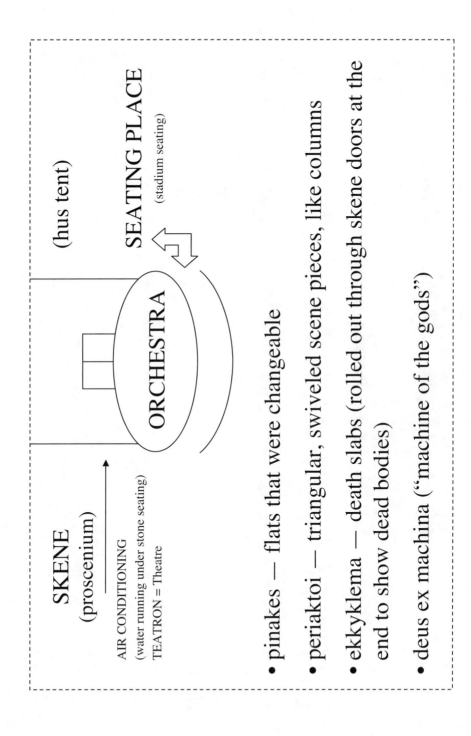

SKENE
(proscenium)

(hus tent)

AIR CONDITIONING
(water running under stone seating)
TEATRON = Theatre

ORCHESTRA

SEATING PLACE
(stadium seating)

- pinakes — flats that were changeable

- periaktoi — triangular, swiveled scene pieces, like columns

- ekkyklema — death slabs (rolled out through skene doors at the end to show dead bodies)

- deus ex machina ("machine of the gods")

ROMAN THEATRE: 300 B.C.

THE REMOTE CONTROL SYNDROME

(competing for audiences—selling out to ratings. Romans thought Greeks were snobbish, uptight; British vs. American analogy)

OTHER EFFORTS TO FIGHT (IN COLISEUM SHOWS):

1. Chariot races

2. Horse racing

3. Foot races

4. Acrobatics

5. Gladiator contests

   (slaves from Britain, Africa made to fight each other for sport)

6. Wild animal fights

   (opening of Coliseum; 9,000 killed) (Christians persecuted)

7. Entertainment wars

8. Boat races and sea battles

   (Coliseum filled with water for sea battles)

ROMAN DRAMA PUT VIOLENCE ON STAGE

Real murders—slaves and criminals were made to act in plays and face the "mouth of hell" (they were executed during the production)

SENECA:
SHAKESPEARE'S INFLUENCE

New Rules for Drama:

1. Five episodes separated by choral: acts with narrator

2. Elaborate speeches: monologue/soliloquy

3. Interest in morality/sensational deeds that illustrate the evils of unrestrained emotion

4. Scenes of violence and horror ONSTAGE

5. Preoccupation with magic, death, human vs. superhuman worlds: *Romeo and Juliet, Hamlet, A Midsummer Night's Dream* show influence

6. Characters with single obsession/passion that drives them to doom

7. Technical devices: soliloquies, asides, confidantes

THE DARK AGES AND MEDIEVAL DRAMA: 476–1453 A.D.

WHY DID IT START?

1. Fall of Roman Empire
2. Rise of Christian Church

- Theatre was considered hedonistic; worship of gods—*bad*

- Church controlled literacy/monks and Latin (all books were written in Latin so only the monks could read)

- There were some leftover traveling pageant plays, but they were chased by the police; actor's social status was very low (literally *criminals*)

Church plays: liturgical dramas to teach lessons

Passion plays: about Christ—life, death, resurrection

Miracle plays: about events in the Bible

Morality plays: about allegories; characters are abstractions and represent all people

At first, only clergy could act; then later, laymen were again allowed to act

THE RENAISSANCE (REBIRTH) BEGINS: 1453

WHY? THE FALL OF CONSTANTINOPLE TO THE TURKS

- Actors and scholars fled to Italy
- There they gave rebirth to classical tradition of literature and drama (*Neoclassicism*)

ITALIAN ARTISTS' STRICT RULES OF DRAMA:

- Five acts
- Tragedies had to teach moral lessons
- All drama is a vehicle of instruction
- Events had to be able to happen in everyday life
- Tragedy with nobility; comedy with middle or low class
- No mixing of tragedy or comedy
- Follow the unities of time, place, action

THE ELIZABETHAN RENAISSANCE

Named for Queen Elizabeth I: Reigned 1558–1603

- Elaborate court masques as precursor: Inigo Jones designed sets (first)

- Legally recognized previously outlawed actors with patronage

- *Patronage:* given a nobleman's name and protection but no money

- Theatre seen as social elite decadence

- Middle class still saw actors as outlaws

- Theatres were not allowed in London city limits

  1. Prevent people from being tempted to leave work and be corrupted

  2. Robbers frequented playhouses

- *However,* the Queen pushed theatre to build unity in the country by having actors portray history. Because Catholics and Protestants were at odds, she tried to bring them together by focusing on historical pride in the country.

WILLIAM SHAKESPEARE— "THE BARD"

- Considered England's greatest dramatist—tragedies, comedies, *and* histories
- Borrowed from the classics/especially Seneca

1. Music   2. Acts   3. Tragic flaws   4. Narrator   5. Violence on stage

- He was an actor, then an author
- Lord Chamberlain's men—became King's men

1. Ten to twenty men, three to five boy apprentices, women characters but no women actors

2. The Globe Theatre
   a. Groundlings
   b. Orange wenches of questionable repute
   c. Atmosphere
   d. 1,000–2,000 spectators
   e. Noise levels demanded attention getting
   f. Playwrights wrote for individual theatres/actors
   g. Rehearsed three to five days and did shows in repertory

OLIVER CROMWELL'S REIGN OF TERROR AND THE RESTORATION

1642–1660: LORD PROTECTOR OF THE COMMONWEALTH

- Puritan: believed theatres were hedonistic, sinful
- Killed Charles I (Charles II and mum fled to France in exile)
- 1660: Restoration (of Charles II to the thrown)

CHARLES II

- Grew up in liberal, artsy France: brought theatre back to England
- Sexual promiscuity both in his life and in theatre
- Introduction of female actors

1. Orange wenches were already in the theatre
2. Women started acting/looking for sugar daddies
3. Nell Gwyn—most famous British actress of the time/Charles II's mistress

- Acting style exaggerated, deliberate
- Fights and love scenes more pronounced—less refined. *People let morals go astray*
- *"Low brow" entertainment:* illicit, sexual, cheap jokes
- Artists ran amok with their new found freedom

SEVENTEENTH- AND EIGHTEENTH-CENTURY DRAMA: THE SEGUE

ENGLAND

- Civil strife during and after Commonwealth
- *After CHARLES II's Restoration period*, playwrights had no money, actors gaining higher status
- Comedy of manners—satirized the social customs of the time
- Middle class fed up with rich; became big audience and pushed melodrama and romanticism
- Teach lessons: hard work wins; laziness loses
- *David Garrick* first serious, realistic actor: he called for more respect from audience—no more sitting on stage

FRANCE

- Molière pushed realism, social commentary
- Costuming became period and not present day
- First time theatre is getting "down to earth" realistic but moving toward *Romanticism*—"nothing is bad"

ROMANTICISM: 1830

CHARACTERISTICS

- Getting rid of neoclassical influence

- Weeding out flowery language

- Love stories/all is well/no problems here

ACTING

- American Touring Company: Edwin Booth (brother of John Wilkes…), John Barrymore and Louise Lane Drew (great-great-grandparents to Drew Barrymore)

- More serious acting (pushed more realism)

- Yet still somewhat presentational, grand

(Why? Big theatre, no sound systems, acoustics, talking audiences)

NINETEENTH- AND TWENTIETH-CENTURY DRAMA: AN OUTGROWTH OF ROMANTICISM

- *Growing distrust of reason:* need to follow instincts to be right

- *Conflicts are mainly man vs. society*

- Melodrama introduced

  – Escapism

  – Good vs. evil with comic relief

- *Sets* had to be historically accurate and individual to the play

- *Actors* becoming socially acceptable as an occupation

- *Playwrights* got copyright protection

ALTERNATIVE THEATRE

SURREALISM

DADAISM

EXISTENTIALISM

(simplistic outlook: "life is meaningless."
More abstract performances and metaphorical)

Picasso (*Surviving Picasso*) wrote many plays—abstract

1. Curtain opens, men with backs to audience. They urinate on the stage, the urine runs to the foot of the stage, they close the curtain.

Themes? How do these differ from previous periods?

REALISM

TURN OF THE CENTURY: WWI AND WWII

THEATRE BECAME ESCAPE FROM STRESS

- See real people overcome odds

- *Ordinary man* overcoming evil or odds

- Became "Everyman" theatre—not elitist

- No more Greek tragedy: evil or fate overcoming superior human

- Wanted real-life portrayal

STANISLAVSKI, GERMANY, AND REALISM

RUSSIAN ACTOR/DIRECTOR

- "Honest portrayal of man in action"
- Cave dweller play: took actors to a cave to live as characters
- Internal vs. external acting; method of physical action
- Physical conventions gave way to psychological motivations

ENSEMBLE ACTING

- *Germany: Duke of Saxe Meiningan* (started ensemble acting)
- Removed "star mentality" (created ensembles)
- Director was given complete vision/authority (first time this arose)
- Actors work together instead of out for themselves

WELL-MADE PLAY

- Cause or problem introduced early
- Effects explored in-depth
- Exposition and plot build to climax
- Suspense
- Logical ending
- Dramatic structure less obvious
- Better construction of story

Some playwrights: George Bernard Shaw, Anton Chekhov, Eugene O'Neill, Tennessee Williams

MODERN DRAMA: A POTPOURRI

NATURALISM

- *Slice of life* (recorded events with no slant/opinion)
- Considered *boring*
- *Emile Zola did films* in this style

ABSURDISM

- No good or bad, only man's perception
- Moral/amoral according to one man's beliefs
- Truth in disorder and chaos (*Waiting for Godot*)

1970s EXPERIMENTAL THEATRE

- Bertolt Brecht, make theatre uncomfortable for audience so they will respond and make changes; alienation
- Poltical/incite activism
- 1970s: Separate audience/tie them to seats/address them directly/throw things on them/alienate them

MUSICAL THEATRE

- Spectacle

- Combined sources: music, dance, dialogue, singing, acting

- Stock musicals (cheese monsters with formula plots)

- Social commentary (*West Side Story and Working*)

- Rock operas (*Jesus Christ Superstar*)

- Modern musicals (*Les Miserables, Phantom of the Opera, Miss Saigon, Titanic, Rent, The Life, Jekyll & Hyde, Hairspray, Side Show, Wicked, The Producers*)

Dramatic Structure Introduction Exercise

LITTLE RED RIDING HOOD: UPDATED

Teacher: Make enough copies for every group. Cut each paragraph out and give one set of paragraphs to each group of students. Have groups put the story into its order. Discuss the elements of dramatic structure: exposition, inciting incident, rising action, climax, falling action, resolution.

There was this girl hanging out in the woods with her mom. She didn't always do the right thing, and she could sometimes get into trouble, but she basically tried to be a good kid. She had a grandmother who lived pretty close, but to get to her house, she had to walk through some scary woods. Her mother told her to go straight there and to come straight home without stopping anywhere.

One day, her mom asked the little girl to go give her grandmother a care package. Because the mother had to work every day to make money because she was the sole breadwinner, the girl had to go by herself. There had been reports about a band of scary robbers, but the mother sent the daughter anyway.

The girl gathered up the care package and her favorite cape and started out on the journey. She hesitated at the foot of the woods because she heard loud and mysterious noises.

When the girl looked back, she saw her mother coming out of the house getting ready to head off to work. The two locked eyes, and her mom didn't look like she was in the mood for a fight, so the girl started walking into the woods.

While walking in the forest, it started to rain, and the care package was getting soaked. The little girl decided to stop in a cave to keep herself and her grandmother's present dry. Although it was dark in there, and her mom had told her not to stop anywhere, she decided to step inside.

Even though her mother had always warned the little girl against playing with matches, she took out a book of matches she'd taken off the stove and lit the match. As she turned to survey the cave, two yellow eyes stared back at her.

As the girl screamed and tried to run out of the cave, she slipped and fell. The yellow eyes were suddenly two inches from her face, and the hot foul breath from a long hairy snout choked each breath the little girl took. Slowly, two ferocious canine teeth were exposed as the dark gray lips on the wolf pulled up and away in a fierce scowl.

The little girl squeezed her eyes tightly closed and braced herself for the inevitable attack, but in another instant, the little girl heard a high pitched yelp and felt a big hand gather her up into strong, reassuring arms.

When she opened her eyes, the girl saw a lumberjack, the man who had been dating her mom. He gently placed her on a rock outside the cave. By that time it had stopped raining, so she was able to sit and recover without worrying about getting wet.

The lumberjack went back inside. Although there was much growling and yelping, the man came back out a few minutes later with a shirt stained as red as the little girl's cape.

After he washed in the creek, the lumberjack walked with the little girl to her grandmother's house. When the old lady opened the door, she saw the blood stained shirt and immediately surmised what had happened. She hugged the lumberjack, gave him some hot food, and tucked the little girl in for a comforting nap.

After the little girl awoke, her mother was there to pick her up. The lumberjack said he would walk with them to keep them safe.

After that day, the mother never again sent her daughter into the woods by herself. She also decided to marry the lumberjack and to keep working. The little girl decided that pushing the rules and getting off the right path could be dangerous to her health, so from that day forward she always did exactly what her mother told her to do.

Aristotle's Dramatic Unities

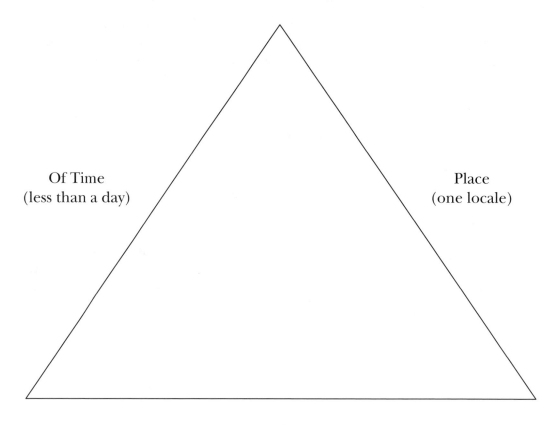

Of Time
(less than a day)

Place
(one locale)

Action
(no subplots)

A play written in the standard dramatic style should include unity of time, place, and action.

Storyboards

The following handout can be used to help students visually identify dramatic structure in a play they are reading, or it may be used to have them create their own plays. The space at the right is for labeling each sketch. Use as many pages as needed to complete the story.

Playwriting Concepts

Plot	Dialogue
Narrative	One-act play
Character	Full-length play
Action	Unity of time
Tone	Unity of action
Beat	Unity of place
Imagery	Exposition
Seed idea	Inciting incident
Rough draft	Rising action
Revisions	Climax
Final draft	Falling action
Monologue	Resolution

Appendix G

Sample Exams:
History and Analysis of Theatre

History and Analysis of Theatre

EXAM #1

ARGUMENT means proving a position or idea with facts. You are expected to back up each opinion you state with proof from your notes, period information in the text, or specific examples from the plays. *You must be completely specific!* If you do not use *facts* to prove the points you claim, you will not receive a favorable grade.

ESSAYS—choose three of the five and write only about those three essays (you can leave two essays out). Please write *so that I can read them.* If your handwriting is not generally readable, please ask to go *type* your answers. (15 points each: 45 total points)

WRITE IN ESSAY FORM. If you do not answer every part of every question, you will not receive full credit.

1. Using specific support from your notes and text (at least five examples), explain:
   a. What political and social trends were in each of the following periods and
   b. Discuss how these trends affected how theatre was produced or used in society in *each period*: Greek, Roman, Medieval, and Renaissance.
2. Choosing two of the three plays studied in class (*Oedipus Rex, Everyman, As You Like It*), using specific examples (at least three for each play), compare and contrast two of the three plays read in class.
   a. How are the plays alike?
   b. How are the two plays different?
3. Using specific examples from your notes and text on the Renaissance and specific examples from *As You Like It* (at least three examples for Greek and three examples for Roman), explain how Shakespeare used elements from both Aristotle's *Poetics* and Seneca's new rules for drama in his writing.
4. Using specific examples (at least two examples of comparisons and at least two examples of contrasts), compare and contrast the Renaissance and the Medieval periods. First explain:
   a. How are the periods alike?
   b. How are the periods different?
   Next explain:
   c. What was the political motivation behind *each* period?
   d. What significant trends developed during each period, *and how* did those trends affect theatre in that time period and today?
   e. What was society's view of theatre at that time?
5. Using at least four specific examples from the play *As You Like It*, explain:
   a. What you consider to be the theme of the play;
   b. What the title, *As You Like It*, has to do with this theme;
   c. And explain why you believe this to be the theme (use your examples from the play here to help prove you are right).

History and Analysis of Theatre

EXAM #2

ARGUMENT means proving a position or idea with facts. You are expected to back up each opinion you state with proof from your notes, period information in the text, or specific examples from the plays. *you must be completely specific!* If you do not use *facts* to prove the points you claim, you will not receive a favorable grade.

ESSAYS—choose three of the five and write only about those three essays (you may leave two essays out). Please write *so I can read them.* If your handwriting is not generally readable, please *type* your answers for the final copy. (15 points each: 45 total points)

WRITTEN ESSAY FORM. If you do not answer every part of every question, you will not receive full credit.

1. Using direct quotes from both the historical information in your text and quotes from both *The Miser* and *The Importance of Being Earnest,* compare and contrast the sixteenth- and seventeenth-century drama period with the eighteenth- and nineteenth-century drama period. Be sure to include the political, social, and dramatic trends. *Use at least five specific examples.*

2. *The Importance of Being Earnest* and *Riders to the Sea* both came from the same period. Please do all of the following:
   a. Identify which period the plays represent.
   b. Explain briefly the philosophies and trends of this period.
   c. Explain how both plays match these philosophies and trends *using specific examples from EACH play.*
   d. Explain at least two specific issues/events that make these plays seem like they are not from the same period.

3. Using specific support from your notes and text (at least five examples), explain:
   a. What political and social trends were in each of the following periods and
   b. Discuss how these trends affected how theatre was produced or used in society in *each period*: sixteenth- and seventeenth-century drama, eighteenth- and nineteenth-century drama, turn-of-the-century realism (*Ghosts*), and 1950s realism (*The Glass Menagerie* and *A Raisin in the Sun*).

4. Using at least four specific examples from the play, *A Raisin in the Sun,* explain:
   a. What you consider to be the theme of the play;
   b. What the title, *A Raisin in the Sun,* has to do with the theme;
   c. Why you believe this to be the theme (use examples from the play here to help prove you are right);
   d. What significance this play had/has for African Americans.

5. Using what you have heard mentioned in class, your class reference booklet, and the information before each play in your text, explain how the development of technology has transformed how plays are produced. Looking at *The Glass Menagerie* and using specific examples, explain:
   a. How lighting would have evolved and made the play more effective;
   b. How set design would be different in a different period (identify the period and explain *in detail* how the set design would be different);
   c. How electricity has changed the production of the play (sound, light, special effects, etc.);
   d. Different examples of subject matter that make this play necessarily take place in the twentieth century;
   e. How the play would be if it were produced before the Industrial Revolution and the invention of several technology instruments (what are those inventions, and how have they changed theatre?).

History and Analysis of Theatre

FINAL EXAM ESSAY: TAKE-HOME TEST

- **Please understand**: *any papers with identical or similar wording will each receive a zero.*
  Please do your own work. You must answer every question (you have one week).
- *Please write all answers in the form of paragraph essays.*

1. Choose two different periods of theatre in which both fall before the twentieth century.
   a. Explain the similarities between these periods and use specific examples to illustrate your point.
   b. Explain the differences between these periods and use specific examples to illustrate your point.
   c. Explain how each period has independently contributed to the field of drama. In other words, why is each period significant? What elements have been adapted in the twentieth century? What are elements that have forever changed the course of theatre? Please explain your answer clearly and with examples.
2. Compare and contrast Modern Realism with Aristotle's rules for drama.
   a. How are the two alike?
   b. How are they different?
   c. Using the characters and situations from both *Oedipus Rex* and *A Raisin in the Sun* or *The Glass Menagerie*, illustrate the differences by explaining the character or theme relationships of each.
3. Compare and contrast musical theatre with twentieth-century drama (straight plays).
   a. What makes these similar?
   b. What makes these different?
   c. What effect does each have on an audience?
   d. What are the different purposes of each type of drama?
   Explain all answers clearly using appropriate examples.
4. Shakespeare is considered to be one of the greatest masterpiece writers.
   a. Explain whether you agree or disagree with that statement.
   b. Give specific examples from any Shakespearean play you have read to prove why you are right. (You may wish to use his style of writing, storylines, poetic nature, etc., to prove your point.)
   Be sure to explain yourself adequately and clearly. You need to build an irrefutable case.
5. Even though *Riders to the Sea* comes from a less realistic period, it has many elements of Modern Realism.
   a. Explain at least three elements or situations from the play that make it realistic.
   b. Explain at least three elements or situations from the play that keep it from being totally realistic.
   Explain all answers clearly using appropriate examples.
6. After having spent a semester studying the history of theatre, explain what you feel to be the four most important aspects/characteristics/benefits of theatre to society.
   Use specific examples to explain your answer.

7. Consider one of the plays read in class this semester.
   a. Using specific examples or support, explain what you feel to be the theme of this chosen play. Be sure the theme is a universal lesson we *all* can learn.
      Be sure to use at least three specific examples that prove your point.
      Be sure to explain yourself adequately and clearly.
8. Pick one of the original plays (not your own).
   a. Name the title.
   b. Explain the characteristics of the period it was trying to emulate.
   c. Explain specifically how this play met the criteria for the period.
   d. Explain specifically the merits of this show (could be special effects, dialogue, plot, dramatic structure).
9. Name the six parts of dramatic structure. Choose a play read in class and detail each part of dramatic structure in that play using specific examples from the script.

History and Analysis of Theatre

FINAL EXAM ESSAY

In-Class Test

Please write clear, multiple paragraph essays for each of the following questions. Please make sure you use facts from your notes or textbooks to help support your ideas. Make sure you give credit to those thoughts that are not yours.

Feel free to use specific plays and dialogue to support your essays.

1. Choose any three elements or techniques of theatre that originated *before* the twentieth century. Explain how and why each was developed, and then explain how each element has been an important part of twentieth-century drama. Use at least two examples per element. (45 points)

2. Starting with Romanticism, outline the major changes in theatre history up through twentieth-century drama. Make sure you include every period studied and explain what makes each period significant. Use at least one detailed example per period. (30 points)

3. Explain the social and political factors that existed in the twentieth century and explain how those factors affected at least three different types of modern drama that developed in the twentieth century. For example, "Because *(this)* was happening in the world, *(this type of theatre)* developed; *(this)* is **why** and **how** it affected twentieth-century theatre." Use at least three detailed examples. (25 points)

Appendix H
Sample Grading Rubrics

PARTNERS _____

_____

Acting Duets

Grading Rubric

BLOCKING

(10) ___ Logical/workable

(10) ___ Logical/workable

(10) ___ Motivated

CHARACTERIZATION

(10) ___ Motivation/intentions (together to build)

(10) ___ Costuming/props (appropriate for scene)

(5) ___ Mood (consistent/appropriate)

(5) ___ Floor plan (effective/logical)

(10) ___ Pacing

DRAMATIC STRUCTURE

(5) ___ Opening clear/definite

(5) ___ Climax

(5) ___ Resolution

(5) ___ Conflict (nicely created/sustained)

Final Exam: Improvisation

Grading Rubric

NAME _____

(10) ___ Characterization (commitment, intensity, appropriate)

(10) ___ Intensions (clear tactics/clear goals)

(15) ___ Dramatic structure (clear beginning, middle, end)

(15) ___ Improvisational techniques (clever, original, creative)

Playwriting Project Rubric*

FOCUS

1	3	5	7	10
Not at all comprehensive; details mostly missing; skeletal script that has disjointed storyline	Somewhat comprehensive; missing many details; skeletal script that has hard-to-follow storyline	Fairly comprehensive; missing some details; somewhat skeletal script that is loosely linked	Mostly comprehensive details; complete storyline	Completely comprehensive; details; complete storyline

ORGANIZATION

1	3	5	7	10
Not at all neat or well arranged; little or no attempt at dramatic structure (DS)	Mostly *not* neat; *not* well arranged; hardly any DS clear	Somewhat neat and well arranged; DS clear but not followed	Mostly neat and well arranged; DS mostly clear	Neat, slick presentation; DS clear and sophisticated

SUPPORT

1	3	5	7	10
Not much substance; little character development	Hardly any substance; little character development	Some substance; character development inconsistent	Mostly quality substance; character development good	All quality substance; character development excellent

CONVENTIONS

1	3	5	7	10
Not very complex or thought out; little regard for period	Hardly complex or thought out; little regard for period	Somewhat complex and thought out; some regard for period but inconsistent	Mostly complex and thought out; mostly regard for period; some inconsistencies	Extra effort; well-planned period; well represented

INTEGRATION

1	3	5	7	10
All elements unequal	Most elements unequal	Some elements unequal	Most elements equal	All elements equal

TOTAL _____

*The categories for this rubric are based on the Illinois Gateway Assessment Program essay grading criteria. Our school district was working to make these criteria thoroughly understandable to students in English and other subjects.

Technology Project Rubric*

FOCUS

1	3	5	7	10
Not at all comprehensive; details mostly missing	Somewhat comprehensive; missing many details	Fairly comprehensive; missing some details	Mostly comprehensive; details	Completely comprehensive; specific details

ORGANIZATION

1	3	5	7	10
Not at all neat or well arranged	Mostly *not* neat; *not* well arranged	Somewhat neat and well arranged	Mostly neat and well arranged	Neat, slick presentation

SUPPORT

1	3	5	7	10
Not much substance	Hardly any substance	Some substance	Mostly quality substance	All quality substance

CONVENTIONS

1	3	5	7	10
Not very complex or thought out; minimal use of technology	Hardly complex or thought out; bare-bones use of technology	Somewhat complex and thought out; adequate use of technology	Mostly complex and thought out; thorough use of technology	Extra effort; well-planned; creative, innovative use of technology

INTEGRATION

1	3	5	7	10
All elements unequal	Most elements unequal	Some elements unequal	Most elements equal	All elements equal

TOTAL _____

*The categories for this rubric are based on the Illinois Gateway Assessment Program essay grading criteria. Our school district was working to make these criteria thoroughly understandable to students in English and other subjects.

Appendix I

Suggested Audition Pieces for Young Actors and Source Guides*

---

*A caution about monologue selection: the best monologues come from those spliced out of quality plays. Make sure you create a strong beginning, middle, and end with one driving theme and strong action. Monologue books can sometimes offer flat or immature pieces that do not have a clear movement and importance.

Twenty Audition Monologues for Women

Play	Playwright	Character	Description	Type
A...My Name is Alice	Kate Shein	Woman	Discussing her hatred of bridal registry	Comedy
And Miss Reardon Drinks a Little	Paul Zindel	Catherine	Explaining why she eats chopped meat	Comedy
And Miss Reardon Drinks a Little	Paul Zindel	Anna	Explaining why dead puppies make her upset	Comedy
Blood Moon	Nicholas Kazan	Manya	Explaining revenge motive against her rapist	Drama
Brighton Beach Memoirs	Neil Simon	Nora	Recounting memories of her father	Drama
Don Juan	Molière	Don Juan's wife	Confronting his cruelty	Drama
Eating Out from 25 Ten Minute Plays	Marcia Dixcy	Chris	Discussing her fight with anorexia	Drama
Eating Out from 25 Ten Minute Plays	Marcia Dixcy	Melanie	Discussing her fight with bulimia	Drama
Eating Out from 25 Ten Minute Plays	Marcia Dixcy	Pat	discussing her fight with diet pills	Drama
Fences	August Wilson	Ruth	Raging against her unfaithful husband	Drama
I Oughta Be in Pictures	Neil Simon	Libby	Discussing her fears with her father	Drama
Jay	Jane Martin	Jay	Discussing her life as a mascot	Comedy
Medea	Christopher Durang	Actress	Introduction monologue welcoming audience	Comedy
Quilt, A Musical Celebration	Jim Morgan, John Schak, and Merle Hubbard	Karen	Crying out against her friend who just died	Drama
Spoon River Anthology	Edgar Lee Masters	Pauline Barrett	Describing her feelings after a double mastectomy	Drama
Table Settings	James Lapine	Alice's sister	Expressing her feelings about her sister	Comedy
The Woolgatherer	William Mastrosimone	Rose	Discussing when she saw boys kill flamingos	Drama
To Gillian on Her 37th Birthday	Michael Brady	Gillian	Reminding David why he needs to keep living	Drama
To Gillian on Her 37th Birthday	Michael Brady	Esther	Fighting with David over his treatment of Rachel	Drama
To Gillian on Her 37th Birthday	Michael Brady	Rachel	Lamenting the death of her mother	Drama

Twenty Audition Monologues for Men

Play	Playwright	Character	Description	Type
Amadeus	Peter Shaffer	Amadeus	Expressing his intense feelings about his music	Serio-comic
Beyond Therapy	Christopher Durang	Stuart	Raving psychiatrist who has had enough from his patient	Comedy
Brighton Beach Memoirs	Neil Simon	Eugene	Discussing his feelings as a teenager	Comedy
Fences	August Wilson	Troy	Raging against his wife about his life	Drama
Inherit the Wind	Jerome Lawrence and Robert E. Lee	Drummond	Addressing the jury with closing arguments	Drama
Little Footsteps	Ted Tally	Ben	Opening monologue about his fear of having kids	Comedy
Man of La Mancha	Dale Wasserman	Cervantes	Discussing what it really means to be crazy	Drama
Tamer of Horses	William Mastrosimone	husband	Raging about his ineffectiveness as a teacher	Drama
Tamer of Horses	William Mastrosimone	Hector	Confessing his horrible childhood	Drama
The Boys Next Door	Tom Griffin	Lucius	Addressing the state government	Drama
The Boys Next Door	Tom Griffin	Arnold	Discussing his frustrations about his job	Comedy
The Glass Menagerie	Tennessee Williams	Tom	Discussing how his sister's memory won't let him go	Drama
The Laramie Project	Moisés Kaufmann	Jedediah	Ruminating about what views are right about Matthew	Drama
The Laramie Project	Moisés Kaufmann	Mr. Shepard	Addressing the court at his son's killer's sentencing	Drama
The Shadow Box	Michael Christofer	Brian	Expressing his anger at his terminal illness situation	Drama
Working	Stephen Schwartz	Charlie	Discussing his life as a pacifist hippie	Comedy
Working	Stephen Schwartz	Ralph	Discussing his enthusiastic patriotism	Comedy
Working	Stephen Schwartz	Mike	Discussing his life as a laborer	Drama
Working	Stephen Schwartz	Conrad	Discussing the fun he can have as a gas man	Comedy
You're a Good Man, Charlie Brown	Clark Gesner	Charlie Brown	Discussing his ineffectiveness as a human being	Comedy

Want to Buy a Book?

POSSIBLE AUDITION MONOLOGUE RESOURCES

Glenn Alterman, *Uptown: Character Monologues for Actors* (A Smith and Kraus Book);
ISBN: 1-880399-08-3.

Jocelyn A. Beard, ed., *The Best Women's Stage Monologues of 1994* (A Smith and Kraus Book);
ISBN: 1-880399-65-2.

Jocelyn A. Beard, ed., *100 Great Monologues from the Neo-Classical Theatre* (A Smith and Kraus Book);
ISBN: 1-880399-60-1.

Jocelyn A. Beard, *One Hundred Women's Stage Monologues from the 1980's* (A Smith and Kraus Book);
ISBN: 0-9622722-9-9.

Richard O. Bell and Joan Kuder Bell, eds., *Auditions and Scenes from Shakespeare* (Theatre Directories);
ISBN: 0-933919-27-1.

Norman A. Bert, ed., *The Scenebook for Actors: Great Monologs & Dialogs from Contemporary & Classical Theatre* (Meriwether Publishing, Limited); ISBN: 0-916260-65-8.

David Black, *The Actor's Audition* (Vintage); ISBN: 0-679-73228-4.

Jerry Blunt, ed., *An Audition Handbook of Great Speeches* (The Dramatic Publishing Company);
ISBN: 1-583420-56-8.

Dick Dotterer, ed., *For Women: Pocket Monologues From Shakespeare* (Dramaline Publications);
ISBN: 0-940669-38-2.

Laura Harrington, ed., "100 Monologues: An Audition Sourcebook" from *New Dramatists,*
(A Mentor Book); ISBN: 0-451-62688-5.

Michael Earley and Philippa Keil, eds., *The Contemporary Monologue: Men* (Routledge);
ISBN: 0-87830-061-9.

Michael Earley and Philippa Keil, eds., *The Contemporary Monologue: Women* (Routledge);
ISBN: 0-87830-060-0.

Michael Earley and Philippa Keil, eds., *Soliloquy! (The Shakespeare Monologues—The Men)* (Applause);
ISBN: 0-93683-978-3.

Michael Earley and Philippa Keil, eds., *Soliloquy! (The Shakespeare Monologues—The Women)* (Applause)
; ISBN: 0-93683-979-1.

Michael Earley and Philippa Keil, eds., *Solo! The Best Monologues of the 80s* (Applause);
ISBN: 0-936839-66-X.

Ginger Howard Friedman, *The Perfect Monologue: How to Find and Perform the Monologue that Will Get You the Part* (Limelight Editions); ISBN: 0-87910-300-0.

Tori Haring-Smith, ed., *Monologues for Women, by Women* (Heinemann); ISBN: 0-435-08630-8.

Roger Karshner, ed., *Monologues from the Classics: Shakespeare, Marlowe and Others* (Dramaline Publications);
ISBN: 0-9611792-7-9.

Eric Kraus, ed., *Monologues from Contemporary Literature*, vol. 1 (A Smith and Kraus Book);
ISBN: 1-880399-04-0.

Jane Martin, *Jane Martin Collected Plays 1980–1995* (A Smith and Kraus Book); ISBN: 1-880399020-2.

Edgar Lee Masters, *Spoon River Anthology* (Collier Books—Macmillan Publishing Company);
ISBN: 0-02-070010-5.

Frank Pike and Thomas G. Dunn, eds., *Scenes and Mono logues from the New American Theater*
(A Mentor Book); ISBN: 0-451-62547-1.

Susan Pomerance, *For Women: Monologues They Haven't Heard* (Dramaline Publications);
    ISBN: 0-9611792-6-0.

Michael Schulman and Eva Mekler, eds., *Great Scenes and Monologues for Actors* (St. Martin's Paperbacks);
    ISBN: 0-312-96654-7.

Nina Shengold & Eric Lane, eds., *Moving Parts: Monologues from Contemporary Plays* (Penguin Books);
    ISBN: 0-14-013992-3.

Michael Shurtleff, *Audition* (Bantam Books); ISBN: 0-553-27295-0.

Marisa Smith and Amy Schewel, eds., *The Actor's Book of Movie Monologues* (Penguin Books);
    ISBN: 0-14-009475-X.

Jack Temchin, ed., *One on One: The Best Women's Monologues for the Nineties* (Applause);
    ISBN: 1-55783-152-1.

POSSIBLE ACTING SCENE RESOURCES

Jocelyn A. Beard, ed., *The Best Stage Scenes of 1994* (A Smith and Kraus Book); ISBN: 1-880399-66-0.

Jocelyn A. Beard, ed., *The Ultimate Scene Study Series (volume two): 102 Scenes for 2 Actors* (A Smith and
    Kraus Book); ISBN: 1-57525-153-1.

Richard O. Bell and Joan Kuder Bell, eds., *Auditions and Scenes from Shakespeare* (Theatre
    Directories); ISBN: 0-933919-27-1.

Norman A. Bert, ed., *The Scenebook for Actors: Great Monologs & Dialogs from Contemporary & Classical
    Theatre* (Meriwether Publishing, Limited); ISBN: 0-916260-65-8.

Alice Childress, *Black Scenes* (Zenith Books—Doubleday); Library of Congress Catalog Card Number:
    70-150881.

Samuel Elkind, ed., *28 Scenes for Acting Practice* (Scot, Foresman and Company).

Samuel Elkind, ed., *30 Scenes for Acting Practice* (Scot, Foresman and Company).

Samuel Elkind, ed., *32 Scenes for Acting Practice* (Scot, Foresman and Company).

John Horvath, Lavonne Mueller, and Hack Temchin, eds., *Duo! Best Scenes for the 90s* (Applause);
    ISBN: 1-55783-030-4.

Frank Pike and Thomas G. Dunn, eds., *Scenes and Monologues from the New American Theater*
    (A Mentor Book); ISBN: 0-451-62547-1.

Michael Schulman and Eva Mekler, eds., *Great Scenes and Monologues for Actors* (St. Martin's Paperbacks);
    ISBN: 0-312-96654-7.

Eric Lane and Nina Shengold, eds., *The Actor's Book of Scenes from New Plays* (Penguin Books);
    ISBN: 0-14-010487-9.

Craig Slaight and Jack Sharrar, eds., *Great Scenes for Young Actors From the Stage* (A Smith and Kraus Book);
    ISBN: 0-9622722-6-4.

John Wray Young, ed., *Audition Scenes for Students* (The Dramatic Publishing Company);
    ISBN: 0-87129-847-3.

Appendix J
Three Character Analysis Ideas

Character Analysis Requirements (#1)

1. Separate each beat (movement of action) in your monologue/scene by drawing a line across the page.
2. Label three columns next to your script: Objective, Why, What.
3. For Objective, describe in an action infinitive verb the overriding objective your character is trying to achieve such as "to wound," "to attack," "to laud," "to honor," "to justify" (something that can be *done*).
4. For Why, explain in detail the tactic or reason behind why the character is trying to achieve the objective.
5. For What, record what you are physically doing—this is where your blocking (stage directions) should be written.

Monologue from King John, Constance, Act III, scene 4

Sample Character Analysis (#1)

Moment Before: She is being condescendingly reproached by Cardinal Pandulph and King John for her sorrowful reaction to the death of her son, thinking she is "mad" or insane:

Cardinal has just said, "Lady, you utter madness, and not sorrow."	OBJECTIVE	WHY YOU NEED THIS	BLOCKING
"Thou art not holy to belie my so; I am not mad: this hair I tear is mine; My name is Constance; I was Geffrey's wife;	To bite back	He is treating me like I have no right to be upset	Turn on him; walk into him, driving her point into his heart
Young Arthur is my son, and he is lost: I am not mad;-I would to heaven I were! For then, 'tis like I should forget myself:	To search for some relief	Madness would be a welcome relief	Stop; face front, arms out welcoming madness
Preach some philosophy to make me mad, and thou shalt be canoniz'd, cardinal;	To spit at/throw his piousness at him	He has no right to govern my grief	Turn; over left shoulder to him
If I were mad, I should forget my son. Grief fills the room up of my absent child. Lies in his bed, walks up and down with me, Puts on his pretty looks, repeats his words, stuffs out his vacant garments with his form; Then have a reason to be fond of grief.	To grasp remnants of memory	It is all that I have left	Wandering DSR as if I'm seeing each new vision
Fare you well: had you such a loss as I, I could give better comfort than you do."	To dismiss him	He's insignificant and unworthy	Calm self; stand straight; slowly face and exit SR

Character Analysis Requirements (#2)

On a separate sheet of paper, answer these questions from your character's point of view.

1. How old are you?
2. List distinctive physical characteristics (such as limp, deformed hands or faces).
3. List all the emotions you go through during this scene or monologue.
4. What do you want most right now?
5. List three ways you are trying to get that (making someone feel guilty, sucking up to someone, etc.).
6. Explain what or who is in your way of getting it.

Character Analysis Requirements (#3)

On a separate sheet of paper, answer these questions from your character's point of view.

1. First name (if it's not in the play, give yourself one)
2. Last name (if it's not in the play, give yourself one)
3. Hair color/style (does not have to/should not be your own)
4. Where do you live? Address/city
5. Social/cultural background
6. Occupation (How rich? What's your financial situation?)
7. Overall attitude toward people
8. Best friend? *(Describe)* Why do you like him or her?
9. What's your favorite hobby?
10. What's your favorite outfit?
11. Why? For the comfort? For the appearance?
12. How much education do you have? *(Be specific)*
13. How intelligent are you?
14. Who is your family? *(Names/relationships)*
15. Pet? What kind and the name? What does the choice of animal say about your character?
16. If you could be anywhere and do anything, where would you go and what would you do?
17. What habits do you have? What expressions?
18. What do you hate more than anything else?
19. What's your secret?

As the actor, step back and look at your answers. What clues do they give as to how to physically, vocally, and mentally play your character?

Appendix K

Technical Request Form

I formed a student technician taskforce that handled all lighting and sound needs for groups that used our auditorium. Having this core collection of students alleviated my having to do all of the technical work for groups other than the drama department.

Technical Request Form

Name _____   Organization _____

Event date _____   Event times _____

Technical requirements:

_____ Lights   _____ Sound   _____ Stage setup

Description of specific needs:

For office use only

Assigned technician(s):

Recorded hours:

Appendix L
Sample Press Releases:
Short and Long Formats

For Immediate Release

MARCH 26, 1998

Macomb High School proudly presents *The Diary of Anne Frank* by Albert Hackett. To be performed April 9 & 10 at 7:30 p.m. and April 11 at 2:30 p.m. in Fellheimer Auditorium at MHS. Tickets at the door. Adults $5; students $3.

FOR IMMEDIATE RELEASE   **CONTACT: JOHN PORTER**

FEBRUARY 24, 2002   PR MANAGER (804) 353-6100

NEW VOICES FOR THE THEATER is proud to announce **YOUNG ACTORS' COMPANY** auditions for the 2002 summer festival.

New Voices for the Theater is looking for eight young actors to fill the prestigious spots in the Young Actors' Company. The auditions will be held in four different locations across the state. A participation fee does apply, and the residency will be held June 30, 2002–July 21, 2002.

Richmond, VA: Auditions will be held Monday, March 18 at TheatreVirginia's Best Products Auditorium from 10 a.m. to 6 p.m. Call Raina Ames at (804) 353-6100 ×212 to schedule an audition time.

Williamsburg, VA: Auditions will be held Tuesday, March 19 at York County School for the Arts from 12 to 5 p.m. Call Raina Ames at (804) 353-6100 ×212 to schedule an audition time.

Leesburg, VA: Auditions will be held Wednesday, March 20 at Loudoun County High School from 12:30 to 5 p.m. Call Raina Ames at (804) 353-6100 ×212 to schedule an audition time.

Blacksburg, VA: Auditions will be held Thursday, March 21 at Virginia Tech's Performing Arts Building, Room 101 from 1 to 6 p.m. Call Raina Ames at (804) 353-6100 ×212 to schedule an audition time.

All auditionees should have one two-minute monologue or two contrasting one-minute monologues. All materials should be from contemporary, published plays. Bring a resume and headshot to the audition.

If auditionees do not have headshots, Polaroid pictures will be taken during the audition time.

Please call Raina Ames, Director of Education & Cooperative Learning, for audition scheduling and information.

Appendix M

Computer Software

Computer Software

- PowerPoint—for classroom lectures/presentations
- Word—for all word processing/typesetting
- Excel—for all database collection
- Publisher—for program/poster creation
- Photoshop—for publicity/program/poster enhancement

Appendix N

Performance and Classroom Contracts

GUYS and DOLLS ACTOR CONTRACT:

Please read the following and then sign in the space provided. Make sure you read this carefully. This is a binding agreement between you and directors:

By signing, you are stating that you understand that just because you audition for one part does not mean the directors are obligated to give you that part. The directors will place you wherever they think you most fit the character and the needs of the directors. You understand that being in the chorus is a big time commitment, but you also know that the lead roles (Sarah, Adelaide, Hotbox Girls, Sky, Nathan, Nicely Nicely, Arvide, Rusty, and Benny, and the Salvation Army band) will require extra rehearsal time. The more lines or songs you have, the bigger your time commitment will be. You understand that you are allowed two (2) absences from rehearsals before the directors have the right to remove you from a scene or replace you all together. Dancers will have to be available Wednesday nights from six until nine o'clock in the evening to work with the choreographer, but the Hotbox Girls and the Crapshooters will have to come to the rehearsals on other days when these scenes and songs are being worked.

In addition, everyone is expected to be in attendance the last ten rehearsals before we open—with no excuses and no questions asked. It takes a lot of work to get a musical ready to perform. You must commit to making this as successful as possible. Each cast member is asked to put in at least ten hours of work on either the set construction or costume coordination, and any extra time you could give would be very much appreciated.

If you wish to be considered for a leading role, you have to understand the time commitment involved. We are asking that anyone cast in a lead rearrange his or her outside schedule to fit musical rehearsals. We will schedule around conflicts as much as possible, but if you are a lead and rehearsal is scheduled during another activity you have, you will have to make the musical the priority. For instance, after solo and ensemble contest is over, you will be asked to rearrange lesson schedules so that you can make it to rehearsals. You absolutely can't come and go to different activities if you are a lead. If we get into that, you will be replaced. If you are not willing or able to make these schedule accommodations, *please do not put yourself up for lead roles.*

All company members are expected to be at every scheduled rehearsal. If you have unexcused absences from rehearsal, you can either be replaced in a number or acting scene, or you may be asked to leave the cast altogether. If you need to go for a doctor's appointment or if you are absent from school, please get word to either Ms. Ames or the stage manager *before* rehearsal begins. If you have many absences whether excused or unexcused that interfere with the running of a scene, you may be replaced with others who don't have as many conflicts.

In terms of sports conflicts, if you are in swimming you will need to make some compromises the first three weeks of musical rehearsal. You may have to leave swim practice early in order to get to musical practice at a certain time. If you are in track, according to the coach, you cannot be in the play at all. If you are in softball or baseball, you cannot be considered for anything more than chorus because your games take you out of school and thus rehearsal time far too many days in any given week. Any other sports you are concerned about need to be talked about with the directors before we cast the show. Any athlete who also wants to be in the musical needs to understand that you have to be at rehearsals when they are scheduled. This means that if you are finished at the sports practice at six o'clock in the evening and have to be at musical rehearsal at the same time, you can't take your time getting there. You may have parents or friends deliver food to you, but you can't drive off and take your time in between these. Therefore, be absolutely sure you want to do both of those activities.

Finally, if you don't get cast in a role that you wanted and you think you will be miserable in the smaller role, please come and talk to us. I would have much more respect you for bowing out of the show instead of staying in and causing trouble with a negative attitude. There are so many good actors and singers, but only one person can be chosen for any given role. We are looking for specific types of performers who have to be able to do certain combinations of things for each of the parts. This does not mean that you are worse than someone else if you don't get cast in a lead. It just might mean you are committed to activities that conflict with rehearsal schedules. It is okay if you make other things your priority, but you have to understand that to put together a quality show, we are going to assemble together those who are most willing or able to make the musical their number one commitment.

_____

(Student signature)

History and Analysis of Theatre Rules Contract*

(Signed portion due September 1 for 20 points' credit)

Because this is an elective course, there is no expectation for discipline problems; however, there is a need for students to be informed *in case* there ever is a problem. Following are the guidelines for class.

RULES

1. Follow all directions the first time
2. Appropriate classroom interaction (allow others to speak uninterrupted, give complete attention to lectures and discussions, relate to others in a positive manner, do not work on other assignments while in History of Theatre)
3. Bring all materials and assignments on time

POSITIVES

1. Praise
2. Special privileges
3. Individual rewards
4. Classwide rewards

CONSEQUENCES

1. First warning (informal teacher conference after class, with pass)
2. Second warning (informal teacher conference after class, no pass)
3. Detention
4. Send to assistant principal

SEVERE CLAUSE

Sent out of the room, immediately receive a detention and a call home

(Please cut and return the bottom portion by September 1)

_____   _____
(Student signature)   (Parent/Guardian signature)

_____

*Contract rules based on Lee Canter discipline principles, a Macomb High School initiative.

Introduction to Play Production Rules Contract*

(Signed portion due September 1 for 20 points' credit)

In a play production class, appropriate behavior is not only doing what assignments you should, but also responding appropriately. A big part of the theatre student's grade is performance; it is impossible for students to feel comfortable participating in a performance class if their peers are making fun of them. Because this is an elective course, I expect that you will be supportive of one another and keep negative comments to yourself. We will deal with problems individually, but below you will find some guidelines for the rules of this class.

RULES

1. Follow all directions the first time
2. Appropriate verbal communication (only making positive remarks; supporting one another, letting everyone have their turn addressing the class without interruption instead of making fun of the student, even jokingly)
3. Appropriate nonverbal communication (clap for each performer; create a supportive environment by facing the front when the performer is on stage, listening attentively, showing interest in students)

POSITIVES

1. Praise
2. Special privileges
3. Individual rewards
4. Classwide rewards

CONSEQUENCES

1. First warning (informal teacher conference after class, with pass)
2. Second warning (informal teacher conference after class, no pass)
3. Detention
4. Send to assistant principal

SEVERE CLAUSE

Sent out of the room, immediately receive a detention and a call home.

No student has the right to disturb the education process for peers or the teacher; furthermore, each performer deserves respect for having the courage to freely share his or her ideas through acting without feeling intimidated. Please keep comments like "shut up," "you're stupid," or "that's dumb/bad" to yourself. I realize people have bad days, but if you have a consistent problem with this, you will receive an automatic detention each time you say these. Keep in mind the communication process does not end with the *saying* of words.

(Please cut and return the bottom portion by September 1)

_____

_____   _____
(Student signature)   (Parent/Guardian signature)

_____
*Contract rules based on Lee Canter discipline principles, a Macomb High School initiative.

Appendix O
Sample Parental Agreement Letter

Dear Parents,

Congratulations! Your student has been cast in the musical. Included in this packet are a rehearsal schedule and a copy of the audition agreement your student signed. *Guys and Dolls* is a very ambitious effort, but we are excited about the cast we have assembled.

There are many details you will want to know about. Following is information we hope will help you better understand what your student has gotten into. First, anyone cast in a musical pays the $25 activity fee. If possible, please have this paid by Friday, February 4, so your student does not have to sit out of rehearsals. If this due date is a problem, please call Raina Ames or Vicki Mayo at 837-2331.

Next, please make careful note of the student audition agreement. There are many expectations we must have to organize fifty actors and twenty technicians. It is vital that students make it to their scheduled rehearsal times. If they miss often, it might become necessary to reassign students' parts to other actors who are better able to consistently be present at rehearsal. In addition, if students miss too often, this causes a huge disruption in the rehearsal process. We need to do whatever it takes to keep the musical running smoothly.

Another requirement for students is grades eligibility. Anyone who is reported as failing or in danger of failing for at least one class makes himself or herself ineligible to rehearse that following week. *If* a student is on the ineligibility or danger of failing list for more than a week, the directors have the right to replace the actor. In addition, if the student is on the failing list the last two weeks before performance, the student is automatically ineligible and must be replaced for the production.

Regarding the rehearsal schedule, on any given day students could be going from singing, acting, and dancing rehearsals. Experience has taught us that three hours a night are necessary to produce a quality performance. The chorus is a very important element of a musical. The chorus creates the atmosphere for the play. Those cast in the chorus may not have to attend every day for all three hours, but when they are called, it is important that they come on time. (When we can't start on time, the directors will still hold students for the allotted time at the end of rehearsals so that they don't lose any rehearsal time. Please understand this if you have to pick up your child.) Working a schedule around fifty different people with a variety of extracurricular activities is very difficult. We cannot avoid every student's conflicts. We have done the best we can to avoid problems, but there will always be conflicts. By accepting a lead role, the student cast in these role has agreed that the musical is his or her priority. We must operate this way to stay on schedule and not make parents wait in the parking lot after rehearsals are over.

We also have not been able to avoid scheduling over the dinner hour. If your student would like to bring a packed dinner, or you would like to deliver food, this is all perfectly acceptable. The auditorium foyer doors will be open so that you may serve your children, but we ask that when students are scheduled for rehearsal, they do not leave the building during the entire scheduled time. Not only is there an issue of students invariably missing their parts on stage, but we are responsible for your student for that scheduled time. Please help stress with your student that for safety reasons they need to stay on campus while under our supervision.

The last ten rehearsals are mandatory. We will begin adding technical elements starting Monday, April 17. In addition, the last week before we open requires a lot of patience and understanding. The technicians work behind the scenes, but they don't start running set/light/sound changes until that last week. The purpose of tech week is to help the technicians smoothly run the show that your students have worked so hard on. The technicians have nine days to get as polished as the actors who have worked for more than two months. Consequently, tech rehearsals can run very long. We don't wish to put your children through undue stress, but tech rehearsals are a necessary part of creating a smooth and polished performance. Parents may organize to feed all cast and crew or choose to individually feed your children during this difficult time; however, please understand that most of the costumes will be rented from Western Illinois University. As part of our contract with them, actors are not allowed to eat or drink anything but water in costume. Most students will have time to get out of costume and eat between scenes, but we want to keep rehearsal running as smoothly as possible while also taking care of your child's nourishment needs. Some parents have organized cast feedings during this week. If you are interested in this, we would much appreciate your assistance.

There is a lot of overwhelming information here. As you can see, putting a musical together is no small feat. We are excited by what this production can be. With the cooperation of parents and students, we can make this a phenomenal experience. If parents would care to assist their students as they put in their tech hours, we need much help with set construction, lighting, costumes and sewing, concessions organization, backstage monitors, and publicity. If you are willing to help with any, please check the spaces below and send the bottom back with your students. Regardless, please sign, detach, and have students return the below statement by Wednesday, February 2. This acknowledges you have read this information.

Thanks for your continued support for the arts,

Raina Ames
Vicki Mayo

(Please detach and return with your student by February 2.)

_____

I have read and understand the commitment my student has made to *Guys and Dolls.*

_____   _____
          (Student signature)   (Parent/Guardian signature)

Areas I/we can offer help:

____ Set construction   ____ Costumes and sewing   ____ Lights   ____ Publicity

____ Concession coordination   ____ Tech week cast/crew feeding   ____ Dressing room monitors

Appendix P

Resources for Teachers

Teacher Resources

- *Teaching Theatre*—periodical
- *Theatre Topics*—periodical
- *Dramatics*—periodical, published by the Educational Theatre Association
- *Youth Theatre Journal*—periodical
- *Theatre Journal*—periodical
- *American Theatre*—periodical
- Educational Theatre Association
- International Thespian Society
- Theatre Communications Group
- American Alliance for Theatre and Education
- Association of Theatre in Higher Education
- National Endowment for the Arts
- National Endowment for the Humanities
- Local arts council
- Local university theatre department

Web Sites

There is a Web site—infoplease.com—where you can do a quick access to encyclopedia and dictionary entries for a variety of topics. There are also different sections for various categories. For instance, there is a section on performing arts that can be accessed at http://infoplease.com/ipea/A0152802.html. Check out the entire Web site. It can provide quick help when looking for information, or your students can find a starting point for their research projects.

Need to buy a script and can't find it? Try http://www.stageplays.com/index.htm

Need quick resources for the history of musical theatre? Try Musical Theatre History Resources: http://www.artslynx.org/theatre/musicals.htm OR http://www.musicalnotes nmore.com.

Want to Buy a Book?
Here Is All the Information You Need for

Possible Play Production Texts

Lisa Abel, project editor, *Theatre: Art in Action* (National Textbook Company); ISBN: 0-8442-5307-3.

Roy A. Beck, William E. Buys, Daniel Fleishhacker, Russell J. Grandstaff, and J. Thomas Sill, *Play Production in High School* (National Textbook Company): Library of Congress Catalog Number: 67-31708.

David Grote, *Theater: Preparation and Performance* (Scot, Foresman and Company): ISBN: 0-673-27190-0.

Jonniepat Mobley, *Play Production Today* (National Textbook Company): Library of Congress Catalog Card Number: 95-67114.

Harry H. Schanker and Katharine Anne Ommanney, *The Stage & School* (Glencoe): ISBN: 0-07-055145-6.

Fran Averett Tanner, *Basic Drama Projects* (Clark Publishing, Inc.); ISBN (soft cover): 0-931054-31-1; ISBN (hardcover): 0-931054-39-7.

Possible History and Play Analysis Texts

Alexander W. Allison, Arthur J. Carr, and Arthur M. Eastman, eds., *Masterpieces of the Drama* (Macmillan Publishing Co., Inc.); ISBN: 0-02-301910-7.

Carl E. Bain, ed., *The Norton Introduction to Literature: Drama* (W.W. Norton & Company, Inc.); ISBN: 0-393-09366-2.

Morton W. Bloomfield and Robert C. Elliott, eds., *Great Plays: Sophocles to Albee* (Holt, Rinehart and Winston, Inc.); ISBN: 0-03-089464-6.

Oscar Brockett and Robert Findlay, *Century of Innovation: A History of European and American Theatre and Drama Since the Late Nineteenth Century* (Allyn & Bacon); ISBN: 0-205-12878-5.

Oscar Brockett, *History of the Theatre* (Allyn & Bacon); ISBN: 0-205-28171-0.

Marshall and Pat Cassady, eds., *An Introduction to Theatre and Drama* (National Textbook Company); ISBN: 0-8442-5100-3.

Laurence Perrine, *Dimensions of Drama* (Harcourt Brace Jovanovich, Inc.); ISBN: 0-15-517655-2.

Melvin R. White and Frank M. Whiting, eds., *Playreader's Repertory: An Anthology for Introduction to Theatre* (Scot, Foresman and Company); Library of Congress Catalog Card Number: 70-116513.

Teacher Resource Books

Donna J. Arnink, *Creative Theatrical Makeup* (Prentice Hall Press); ISBN: 0-13-191305-0.

Greg Atkins, *Improv!: A Handbook for the Actor* (Heinemann); ISBN: 0-435-08627-8.

David Ball, *Backwards & Forwards: A Technical Manual for Reading Plays* (Southern Illinois University Press); ISBN: 08-93-1110-0.

Robert Benedetti, *The Actor in You: Sixteen Simple Steps to Understanding the Art of Acting* (Allyn & Bacon); ISBN: 0-205-26999-0.

Philip Bernardi, *Improvisation Starters: A Collection of 900 Improvisation Situations for the Theater* (Betterway Books); ISBN: 1-55870-233-4.

Anne Bogart, *A Director Prepares: Seven Essays on Art and Theatre* (Routledge); ISBN: 0-415-23831-5.

Richard Brestoff, *The Great Acting Teachers and Their Methods* (A Smith & Kraus Book); ISBN: 1-57525-012-8.

Dennis Brown, *SHOPTALK: Conversations about Theater and Film with Twelve Writers, One Producer and Tennessee Williams' Mother* (Newmarket Press); ISBN: 1-55704-170-9.

Richard Corson and James Glavan, *Stage Makeup* (Allyn & Bacon); ISBN: 0-13-606153-2.

Bernard F. Dukore, *Dramatic Theory and Criticism: Greeks to Grotowski* (Harcourt Brace Jovanovich College Publishers); ISBN: 0-03-091152-4.

C. J. Gianakaris, *Foundations of Drama* (Houghton Mifflin Company); ISBN: 0-395-18611-0.

Patti P. Gillespie and Kenneth M. Cameron, *Western Theatre: Revolution and Revival* (Macmillan); ISBN: 0-02-343050-8.

J. Michael Gillette, *Theatrical Design and Production: An Introduction to Scene Design and Construction, Lighting, Sound, Costume, and Makeup* (McGraw-Hill Companies); ISBN: 0-07-256262-5.

Burnet M. Hobgood, ed., *Master Teachers of Theatre: Observations on Teaching Theatre by Nine American Masters* (Southern Illinois University Press); ISBN: 0-8093-1464-9.

Alison Hodge, ed., *Twentieth Century Actor Training* (Routledge); ISBN: 0-415-19452-0.

Richard Hornby, *The End of Acting: A Radical View* (Applause); ISBN: 1-55783-213-7.

J. D. Martinez, *Combat Mime: A Non-Violent Approach to Stage Violence* (Nelson-Hall Publishers); ISBN (cloth): 0-88229-730-9; ISBN (paper): 0-88229-809-7.

Bruce A. McConachie, *Interpreting the Theatrical Past* (University of Iowa Press); ISBN: 0-87745-238-5.

Bruce A. McConachie, *Melodramatic Formations: Studies in Theatre History and Culture* (University of Iowa Press); ISBN: 0-87745-360-8.

Eric Morris and Joan Hotchkis, *No Acting Please: "Beyond The Method" A Revolutionary Approach to Acting and Living* (Ermor Enterprises Publishing); ISBN: 0-9629709-3-X.

Maria C. Novelly, *Theatre Games for Young Performers: Improvisations & Exercises for Developing Acting Skills* (Meriwether Publishing Ltd.); ISBN: 0-916260-31-3.

Janelle G. Reinelt and Joseph R. Roach, eds., *Critical Theory and Performance* (The University of Michigan Press); ISBN: 0-472-09458-0.

Viola Spolin, *Improvisation for the Theater* (Northwestern University Press); ISBN: 0-8101-4000-4.

Viola Spolin, *Theater Games for Rehearsal: A Director's Handbook* (Northwestern University Press); ISBN: 0-8101-4002-2

Constantine Stanislavski, *An Actor's Handbook* (Theatre Arts Books); ISBN: 0-87830-509-2.

Lawrence Stern, *Stage Management* (Allyn & Bacon); ISBN: 0-20-533531-4.

Laura Thudium, *Stage Makeup: The Actor's Complete Step-by-Step Guide to Today's Techniques and Materials* (Watson-Guptill Publications); ISBN: 0823088391.

Melvin R. White, *Mel White's Readers Theatre Anthology* (Meriwether Publishing Ltd.); ISBN: 0-916260-86-0.

Harry K. and Rosemary Tripi Wong, *The First Days of School: How To Be An Effective Teacher* (Harry K. Wong Publications, Inc.); ISBN: 0962936065

Classroom/Forensics Resources

"THE NEW CLASSICS"

Multicultural Plays and Contemporary Classics:

- *F.O.B.* by David Henry Hwang
- *Yankee Dawg You Die* by Philip Kan Gotanda
- *I Don't Have to Show You No Stinking Badges!* in the book *Zoot Suit and Other Plays* by Luis Valdez
- *The Colored Museum* by George C. Wolfe
- *Santos y Santos* by Octavio Solis
- *'Night Mother* by Marsha Norman
- *Marisol* by Jose Rivera
- Nilo Cruz (Cuban-American playwright out of The New Theatre in Florida)
- *Yellowman* by Dael Orlandersmith
- *Darker Face of the Earth* by Rita Dove (updated *Oedipus Rex* set in the slavery era)
- *Jails, Hospitals, and Hip Hop* by Danny Hoch
- *Some People* by Danny Hoch
- *Dancing on Moonlight* by Keith Glover
- *African Company Presents Richard III* by Carlyle Brown
- *Wit* by Margaret Edson
- *Top Dog/Underdog* by Suzan-Lori Parks
- *Angels in America* by Tony Kushner
- *For Colored Girls Who Have Considered Suicide When the Rainbow Is Enuf* by Ntozake Shange
- *For Colored Boys Who Have Considered Homicide* by Narcel Reedus
- *The Laramie Project* by Moisés Kaufman and members of the Tectonic Theatre Project
- *Six Degrees of Separation* by John Guare
- *The Heidi Chronicles* by Wendy Wasserstein
- *Lion in Winter* by James Goldman

Some Things to Check Out for Forensics Events

- *Tamer of Horses* by William Mastrosimone (the scene in which the teacher is trying to get the student to ask for an orange without words and the boy erupts in violence, thereby proving the teacher's point that words and literacy are the only things that will bring the student out of his cycle of violence and crime)
- Gwendolyn Brooks' *Children Coming Home*, a series of poems written about inner-city kids who are facing many obstacles and challenges
- *The Day the Bronx Died* by Michael Henry Brown

Script Sources

ROYALTIES AND SCRIPTS: MUSICALS

Music Theatre International: http://www.mtishows.com/
The Rogers & Hammerstein Theatre Library: http://www.rnh.com/theatre/
Tams-Witmark: http://www.tams-witmark.com/

ROYALTIES AND SCRIPTS: PLAYS

Anchorage Press Plays, Inc.: http://www.applays.com/
P.O. Box 2901, Louisville, KY 40201-2901
Phone/fax: (502) 583-2288
E-mail: applays@bellsouth.net

Baker's Plays: http://www.bakersplays.com/store/
P.O. Box 699222
Quincy, MA 02269-9222
Phone: (617) 745-0805
Fax: (617) 745-9891

Broadway Play Publishing, Inc.: http://www.broadwayplaypubl.com/
56 E. 81st
New York, NY 10028-0202
Phone: (212) 772-8334
Fax: (212) 772-8358

Dramatic Publishing: http://www.dramaticpublishing.com/
P.O. Box 129
Woodstock, IL 60098-0129
Phone: 1-800-448-7469
Fax: 1-800-334-5302

Dramatists' Play Service, Inc.: http://www.dramatists.com/index.asp
440 Park Avenue, South
New York, NY 10016
Phone: (212) 683-8960
Fax: (212) 213-1539
E-mail: postmaster@dramatists.com

Samuel French, Inc.: http://www.samuelfrench.com/

45 West 25th Street—Dept. W   7623 Sunset Blvd.—Dept. W
New York, NY 10010   Hollywood, CA 90046
Phone: (212) 206-8990   Phone: (323) 876-0570
Fax: (212) 206-1429   Fax: (323) 876-6822

Items to Stock in Your Scene Shop

Fine wood dining table/matching chairs

Hutch

Settee

Kitchen cabinets

Fake books/television/radio

Artificial flowers/plants

Urns

Railings

Stock staircases (tall and short—preferably to fit ready-made platforms)

Ramps

Molding

Lattice work

Dollies (to move heavy pieces—you can use standard moving dollies, or the scooters used in gym class work really well. If the physical education department can spare some, four are great for moving heavy pieces)

Multiple cubes (in different sizes)

Masking flats (black flats)

Stock flats (standard 4' × 8', 4' × 10', 4' × 12' with two-foot-wide flats at matching heights; some solid, some with windows, some with doors)

4' × 8' platforms

Costume racks/storage wardrobes and cabinets

Tree stands for lights

Makeup supplies

Shows that Work Well with
High School Students*

MUSICALS

Annie
Anything Goes
Beauty and the Beast
Brigadoon
Hello Dolly!
Fiddler on the Roof
Follies
Funny Girl
Guys and Dolls
Honk!
How To Succeed in Business without Really Trying
Into the Woods
Kiss Me Kate
Mame
Oklahoma
Peter Pan
Schoolhouse Rock Live!
Seven Brides for Seven Brothers
The Music Man
The Sound of Music
West Side Story
Wind in the Willows
Working

PLAYS

A Christmas Carol
And Then They Came For Me
Antigone
As You Like It
A Woman Called Truth
Beau Jest
Brighton Beach Memoirs
Dracula
Fools
Little Footsteps
Much Ado About Nothing
Spoon River Anthology
Tender Lies
The Crucible
The Diary of Anne Frank
The Foreigner
The Importance of Being Earnest
The Lark
The Miracle Worker
To Gillian on Her 37th Birthday
Up the Down Staircase
Wait until Dark
You Can't Take It with You

---

*Raina Ames, *Master Class: Directing the Musical Brainstorming List*, NETC, 2004.

Appendix Q
Sample Blocking Notation

Blocking Abbreviations

Back Wall

USR Upstage Right	USC Upstage Center	USL Upstage Left
SR Stage Right	CS Center Stage	SL Stage Left
DSR Downstage Right	DSC Downstage Center	DSL Downstage Left

AUDIENCE

Stage directions are referred to as *upstage/downstage* because the early stage floors used to be raked (slanted), so actors had to walk "up" to go toward the back wall, and they had to walk "down" to go toward the audience.

Left/right is from the actor's point of view as he or she stands looking toward the audience.

↷ = C Cross
X = Cross to
→ = X SR to (e.g., Benedick → Beatrice)
← = X SL to (e.g., Benedick ← Beatrice)

Give each entrance a number so you can reference easily (#1, #2, #3, etc.)

Excerpt from *Much Ado About Nothing* by William Shakespeare
Sample Blocking Script Notation

(1) *Exuent Pedro, Claudio and Leonato* Benedick: *(coming forward)* This can be no trick. The conference was sadly bourne. They have the truth of this from Hero. They seem to pity the lady. It seems her affections have their full bent. **(2)** Love me? Why, it must be requited. I hear how I am censured. They say I will bear myself proudly, if I perceive the love come from her; **(3)** they say too that she will rather die than give any sign of affection. I did never think to marry. I must not seem proud; happy are they that hear their detractions and can put them to mending. They say the lady is fair; **(4)** 'tis a truth, I can bear them witness; and virtuous, 'tis so, I cannot reprove it; and wise but for loving me; by my troth, it is not addition to her with, nor no great argument or her folly, for I will be terribly in love with her. **(5)** I may chance have some odd quirks and remnants of wit broken on me, because I have railed so long against marriage. But doth not the appetite alter? Shall quips and sentences and these paper bullets of the brain awe a man from the career of his humor?	**(1) They exit out #3 while Benedick crawls along and watches them go—gets on knees collapsing on round bench** **(2) stand—SR of round bench** **(3) USL of round bench** **(4) in a daze—tries to lean into shrub; hand gets pricked—rubs hand—sits on USL of round bench—swings legs into center and face DSR** **(5) sink into center of round bench**
(6) No, the world must be peopled! When I said I would die a bachelor, I did not think I should live till I were married. **(7)** Here comes Beatrice. By this day, she is a fair lady! *Enter Beatrice*	**(6) stands in center of round bench** **(7) struggles to get out as BEA enters #1**
Beatrice: **(8)** Against my will I am sent to bid you come to dinner. Benedick: **(9)** Fair Beatrice, I thank you for your pains. Beatrice: I took no more pains for those thanks than you take pains to thank me. If it had been painful, I would not have come. **(10)** Benedick: You take pleasure in the message? Beatrice: Ye, just so much as you may take upon a knife's point. **(11)** You have no stomach, signor? Fare you well. **(12)** *Exits away from others*	**(8) she stops on platform at the stairs** **(9) X USR to stairs, foot up on one** **(10) turns to go—he is up on platform in front of her** **(11) she tries to get past; he blocks her** **(12) she goes down steps and out #4**
Benedick: Ha! "Against my will I am sent to bid you come to dinner." There's a double meaning in that. "I took no more pains for those thanks than you took pains to thank me." That's as much to say, "Any pains that I take for you is as easy as thanks." If I do not pity her, I am a villain; If I do not lover her, I am a rascal. I will go get her picture. **(13)**	**(13) he follows her out #4**

For each new page, start over at #1.

Appendix R

Sample Shakespeare Script Cuttings
Examples from *A Midsummer Night's Dream*

Shakespeare's subplots need not be cut to shorten the play for youth theatre. However, streamlining the script to get more succinctly to the meaning is an appropriate measure. In *A Midsummer Night's Dream* when Egeus makes his first entrance, his speech is packed with metaphors and descriptions. These only bog down a young actor who is not yet able to finesse such long-winded verse. The original speech is written as:

> Full of vexation come I, with complaint
> Against my child, my daughter Hermia.
> Stand forth, Demetrius. My noble lord,
> This man hath my consent to marry her.
> Stand forth, Lysander. And my gracious duke,
> This hath bewitch'd the bosom of my child.
> Thou, thou, Lysander, thou hast giv'n her rhymes
> And interchanged love-tokens with my child;
> *Thou has by moonlight at her window sung*
> *With feigning voice verses of feigning love,*
> *And stol'n the impression of her fantasy*
> *With bracelets of thy hair, rings, gauds, conceits,*
> *Knacks, trifles, nosegays, sweetmeats-messengers*
> *Of strong prevailment in unhardened youth.*
> With cunning hast thou filch'd my daughter's heart.
> Turn'd her obedience (which is due to me)
> To stubborn harshness. And, my gracious duke,
> Be it so she will not here before your grace
> Consent to marry with Demetrius,
> I beg the ancient privilege of Athens:
> As she is mine, I may dispose of her,
> Which shall be either to this gentleman
> Or to her death, according to our law
> Immediately provided in that case.

Without marring the basic meaning, the edited version shapes out as:

> Full of vexation come I, with complaint
> against my child, my daughter Hermia.
> Stand forth, Demetrius. My noble lord,
> this man hath my consent to marry her.
> Stand forth, Lysander: and my gracious duke,
> this hath bewitch'd the bosom of my child.
> Thou, thou, Lysander, thou hast giv'n her rhymes,
> and interchang'd love-tokens with my child:
> With cunning hast thou filch'd my daughter's heart.
> Turn'd her obedience, which is due to me,
> to stubborn harshness: and, my gracious duke,
> be it so she will not here before your grace
> consent to marry with Demetrius,
> I beg the ancient privilege of Athens:
> as she is mine, I may dispose of her,
> which shall be either to this gentleman
> or to her death, according to our law
> immediately provided in that case.

This text cuts to the bone of the issue: the complaint, the charge against Lysander, and the request for punishment; the deeper description is left out to make the story more clear both to the actor and to the audience. Capital letters have been removed from the beginnings of some lines and punctuation has been changed to lessen the likelihood that young actors will fall into a sing-song rhyming lilt. This alteration in type style and format will aid actors greatly in talking through to the end of punctuation and finding a more natural speaking pattern for Shakespeare's different words and style of speaking.

In editing the Shakespearean script, it is essential that every scene be evaluated for what is absolutely necessary; any extraneous or repeated dialogue should be cut. For example, Oberon's character: his speeches are beautiful poetry, but young actors often have a difficult time bringing these words alive. By cutting the speeches down to the core of the through line (the character's one driving motivation), students are able to not only grasp the meaning more easily but they also are able to drive the action more clearly. In Act II, Scene 1, Oberon waxes on:

OBERON

> Well, go thy way: thou shalt not from this grove
> Till I torment thee for this injury.
> My gentle Puck, come hither. Thou rememb'rest
> *Since once I sat upon a promontory*
> *And heard a mermaid, on a dolphin's back,*
> *Uttering such dulcet and harmonious breath*
> *That the rude sea grew civil at her song,*
> *And certain stars shot madly from their spheres*
> *To hear the sea-maid's music?*

PUCK

> I remember.

OBERON

> That very time I saw (but thou couldst not)
> Flying between the cold moon and the earth
> Cupid, all arm'd. A certain aim he took
> At a fair vestal, throned by the west,
> And loosed his love-shaft smartly from his bow,
> As it should pierce a hundred thousand hearts.
> But I might see young Cupid's fiery shaft
> Quenched in the chaste beams of the wat'ry moon,
> And the imperial vot'ress passed on,
> In maiden meditation, fancy-free.
> Yet marked I where the bolt of Cupid fell.
> It fell upon a little western flower,
> Before milk-white, now purple with love's wound,
> And maidens call it love-in-idleness.
> Fetch me that flower; the herb I shewed thee once.
> The juice of it, on sleeping eye-lids laid,
> Will make or man or woman madly dote
> Upon the next live creature that it sees.
> Fetch me this herb, and be thou here again
> Ere the leviathan can swim a league.

PUCK

> I'll put a girdle round about the earth
> In forty minutes.

Although these passages paint beautiful pictures for the listener, a less experienced actor benefits more from cutting to the heart of the matter:

OBERON

> Well, go thy way: thou shalt not from this grove
> till I torment thee for this injury.
> *(Puck starts to back away quietly from Oberon)*
> My gentle Puck, come hither. Thou rememb'rest
> Cupid all arm'd: a certain aim he took
> at a fair vestal throned by the west
> and loosed his love-shaft smartly from his bow.

PUCK

> I remember.

OBERON

> It fell upon a little western flower,
> before milk-white, now purple with love's wound.
> Fetch me that flower; the herb I shew'd thee once.
> The juice of it on sleeping eye-lids laid
> will make or man or woman madly dote
> upon the next live creature that it sees.

PUCK

> I'll put a girdle round about the earth
> in forty minutes.

Shakespearean productions can be valuable experiences for young actors. If scripts are edited properly, both actors and audience will make sense of the story and Shakespeare will come alive in a vibrant and exciting way for all involved. For easy editing, find the complete text online so you can save it as a digital file.

Speaking Shakespeare's Text*

1. When the words are written in verse, map out the iambic pentameter (ten beats per line) to signal which words are most important to the text:

/   /   /   /   /

Thou, thou, Lysander, thou hast giv'n her rhymes,

/   /   /   /   /

And interchang'd love-tokens with my child

The stressed words become the operatives in each phrase, calling for more stress *without* getting caught in the sing-song rhythm of iambic pentameter. *Understand that sometimes in iambic pentameter, some syllables are shortened in order to make the words fit into the meter. Try to stay true to this as much as possible. Sometimes iambic pentameter is broken or there are too many syllables in a line.* This signals an upset in the harmony, and you should use this as a cue toward what is happening with characters at that given moment. Sometimes, in extreme emotional moments, the perfect flow of the rhythm is disturbed. Use this to your fullest effect as an actor—*but note that "lower class" characters often speak in prose, not poetry.*

2. If a word is written without an apostrophe taking the place of a letter, you *do* pronounce that syllable *as separate from the rest of the word*; however, if an apostrophe is included, you *do not* separate that syllable from the rest of the word.

   Example: interchang'd is spoken as three syllables, but interchanged is spoken as four syllables.

3. Drive through to the end of a thought. If there is *no* end punctuation finishing a line, speak through until you reach **end** punctuation.

4. Paraphrase lines and know the meanings of unfamiliar words so you can make the lines intelligible both to you and to your audience.

5. Do not try to add any lofty speech patterns to Shakespeare. Realize that phrases used were accepted in every day language. The only difference is that Shakespeare was writing in poetical form as an art. As an actor, you do not have to make your performance "artsy." The success is in making Shakespeare's words sound as conversational as possible *in spite of* the heightened language.

6. Any time there is a string of three items, each is meant to be given more stress than the last so that one builds more on the other. Such triplets add rhythm and drive the energy of the performance.

   Example: and she, sweet lady, *(1) dotes,*
   (2) devoutly dotes, (3) dotes in idolatry
   upon this spotted and inconstant man.

---

*Ideas modified from Dr. Daniel L. Calvin's dramaturgical work with Macomb High School's *Much Ado About Nothing*.

BIBLIOGRAPHY

Hobgood, Burnet, ed. *Master Teachers of Theatre*. Illinois: Southern Illinois University Press, 1988

SELECTED BIBLIOGRAPHY

Abel, Lisa, ed. *Theatre: Art in Action*. Illinois: National Textbook Company, 1999.

Bogart, Anne. *Director Prepares*. New York: Routledge, 2001.

Brestoff, Richard. *The Great Acting Teachers and Their Methods*. New Hampshire: Smith & Kraus, Inc., 1995.

Brockett, Oscar. *History of Theatre*, 9th edition. Massachusetts: Allyn & Bacon, 2002.

Canter, Lee. *Assertive Discipline Workbook 6-12*. California: Canter & Associates, Incorporated, 1992.

Corson, Richard and James Glavan. *Stage Makeup, 9th edition*. Massachusetts: Allyn & Bacon, 2001.

Grote, David. *Play Directing in the School: A drama director's survival guide*. Colorado: Meriwether Publishing, Ltd., 1997.

Kissel, Howard, ed. *Stella Adler: The Art of Acting*. New York: Applause Theatre & Cinema Book Publishers, 2000.

Miller, Bruce J. *The Actor as Storyteller: An Introduction to Acting*. California: Mayfield Publishing Company, 2000.

Novelly, Maria C. *Theatre Games For Young Performers: Improvisations & Exercises for Developing Acting Skills*. Colorado: Meriwether Publishing, Ltd, 1985.

Schanker, Harry H. *The Stage and School, Student Edition*. New York: Glencoe/McGraw-Hill, 2004.

Spolin, Viola. *Theatre Games For Rehearsal: A Director's Handbook*. Illinois: Northwestern University Press, 1985.

Stern, Lawrence. *Stage Management*, 7th edition. Massachusetts: Allyn & Bacon, 2001.

Wong, Harry K. and Rosemary Tripi Wong. *The First Days of School: How To Be An Effective Teacher* California: Harry K. Wong Publications, Inc., 2004.

INDEX

A

Abel, Lisa, 13
Actors, 12; *see also* Casting
    technical work requirements, 6
    training methods, 26
Adler, Stella, 26, 40
Administrator–teacher relationships, 17–18
    value of saying "no," 21–22
Assertive Discipline, 8
Assignments, 13
Attendance requirements, 36
Auditions, 9, 34, 36
Audition sheets, 36

B

Back of the house technicians, 30–31
Booster clubs, 25
Brandwein, Michael, 4
Brockett, Oscar, 5, 40

C

Canter, Lee, 8
Casting
    consistent guidelines for, 33–34
    criticisms of, 34
    favoritism, 8–9, 15–16, 35
    issues in, 33–36
    program objectives and, 33
    stage manager and, 30
    standards for auditions, 36
    student overextension, 35
    understudies, 35
    use of same actor, 35
Chaperones, 15–16, 34
Chapman, Clay McLeod, 6
Character analysis, 12
Classroom environment
    order in, 8
    professionalism in, 8–10
    rules for, 8
    style of discipline, 8–20

Class syllabus, 13
Costume changers, 31
Costume design, 11–12, 28, 31

D

Detention, 38
Diary of Anne Frank, The (Goodrich and Hackett), 41
Directing projects, 6, 12, 42
Director's books, 12
Discipline problems, 7–10, 38
Drama programs, *see* Theatre curriculum
    business/financial aspects of, 26–27
    planning for, 29
    publicity for, 28
    strengthening your program, 25
    technical needs of, 29

E

Educational Theatre Association, 25
Ethical issues, 37–38
Extracurricular activities
    pressure by administrators, 21–22
    program responsibilities, 12–13, 21–22
    scheduling conflicts, 23–25

F

Favoritism, 8–9, 15–16, 35
First Days of School: How To Be An Effective Teacher, The (Wong and Wong), 8
Fund-raisers, 25

G

Goodrich, Frances, 41
Grading, 13
Greek theatre, 5

H

Hackett, Albert, 41
"History and Analysis of Theatre" course, 5, 13

History of Theatre (Brockett), 5

I
Improvisations, 12, 41
International Thespian Society, 25
Introduction to Theatre & Drama, An, 5

J
Job burnout, 22
Joyce, Maxine, 39

L
Lighting design, 12, 29–30

M
Makeup techniques, 6, 11–12, 31
Monologues, 6, 12–13
Motivation of students, 4
Musical productions, 25

N
Novelly, Maria, 12

P
Parent relationships, 15–16
Parent volunteers, 16
Performance pieces, 4, 13
Playbill, 28–29
Play competitions, 24
Play production class, extracurricular program
        and, 12
Play Production Today, 13
Playwright-in-Residence, 5
Playwriting skills, 5–6
Press releases, 28
Professional development, 6
Professionalism, 8–10
Programs and posters, 28
Property master, 30
Props, 12
Publicity, 28

R
Rehearsals, 18, 29

S
Scene books, 13
Scene construction, 11–12
Scheduling conflicts, 23–25
Set design/construction, 6, 11–12, 27
        woodworking class and, 6

Shakespeare, 40
Sound boards, 30
Spolin, Viola, 12
Stage crews, 29–31
Stage Management (Stern), 30
Stage managers, 30–31
Stage and School, The, 13
Stern, Lawrence, 30
Strasberg's Method, 26
Students
        inter-personal relationships, 37–38
        ownership of education, 41
        resistance of, 7–8
        scheduling conflicts of, 26

T
Technical crew, 30–31
Tech request form, 31
Textbooks, 13–14
Theater: Production and Performance, 13
Theatre: Art in Action (Abel), 13
Theatre curriculum, 11–13
        benefits of, 3
        concepts of, 4
        developing a, 3–6
        as educational program, 3–4
        factors for success, 41
        historical framework for, 5
        relevancy and respect for, 11
        school's needs and, 4
        in secondary education, 41
Theatre games, 12
Theatre history, 5
Theatre productions, 4, 6, 11
        maintaining excellence of, 39–42
        quality of, 39
Theatre teachers
        ethical issues of, 37–38
        goals of, 40
        personal philosophy of, 4
        responsibilities of, 3–4
        scope of expectations, 40
        teaching assignments, 10
        as team players, 17–18
TheatreVirginia, 5
Time management, 23

U
Understudies, 35

W
Wong, Harry K., 8
Wong, Rosemary Tripi, 8

DATE DUE

12-18-10			
1/3/17			
5/11/19			

Demco, Inc. 38-293